Stephanie Christie-Carmichael is a consultant [...] over 17 years' experience in dealing exclu[...] succession & Inheritance Tax planning for [...] and estate administration across mainland UK.

Stephanie was born and raised in Glasgow, Scotland. Stephanie studied Business Law and graduated with a BA Hons from the University of Strathclyde before returning to complete her LLB and Post Graduate Diploma in Legal Practice.

Stephanie started her career in private practice before moving in house to global accountancy firm, Mazars. From there, she became Managing Director with EBS Trustees Limited, one of Scotland's oldest Will writing & private trust companies, before returning to private practice in 2020 as a Consultant Solicitor.

As well as being a current member of the Law Society of Scotland, Stephanie is also a Notary Public and a full member of STEP (The Society of Trusts and Estates Practitioners), an internationally recognised association for private client professionals. Stephanie has also attained STEP diplomas in both Scottish and English Wills, Trusts and Estates as well as STEP's English Advanced Certificate in Will Writing which was obtained with distinction.

Stephanie's first book "How to Settle an Estate in Scotland – a Practical Guide" was published in 2021 and is available from Law Brief Publishing, Amazon and all good book shops.

A well-known face in the West of Scotland business community, Stephanie is also a regular contributor to Quality Radio's "Legal Matters" program.

Connect with Stephanie via Social Media at:

LinkedIn – www.linkedin.com/in/stephaniechristiecarmichael

Instagram – @stephaniechristiecarmichael

A Practical Guide to Administering Estates and Obtaining Probate in England & Wales

A Practical Guide to Administering Estates and Obtaining Probate in England & Wales

Stephanie Christie-Carmichael
BA (Hons), LLB (Scots), Dip LP, NP, TEP

Law Brief Publishing

Published 2023 by Law Brief Publishing, an imprint of Law Brief Publishing Ltd
30 The Parks
Minehead
Somerset
TA24 8BT

www.lawbriefpublishing.com

Paperback: 978-1-912687-24-4

For my niece, Olivia

Nulla tenaci invia est via

So let your star shine brightly

PREFACE

If you are looking for a book on the history of succession law, a treatise on section so and so of an Act of Parliament or a dissemination of how we arrived at a particular principal of law through common law, I recommend that you stop what you are doing, turn to the back of this book, look at the further reading section and pick a book from there. This is absolutely not going to be the book for you! If you are looking for a book that deals with the practical nuts and bolts of administering an estate in England & Wales and cuts through the legislative and case law red tape, I invite you to please read on!

This book is designed to give law students, general practitioners and solicitors & trainee solicitors who don't normally deal with estates and find themselves for whatever reason thrust into the Private Client world, a guide to dealing with the practical and effective administration of an estate in England and Wales. It will not (and indeed cannot) cover everything you may come across in an estate but it should give you enough information to at least be comfortable managing an average estate on behalf of a client and provide you with sign posts on where to look for further information.

The law stated in this book was believed to be accurate at 1st December 2022.

Stephanie Christie-Carmichael
January 2023

ACKNOWLEDGEMENTS

Before we get down to business, some thanks are due for the people who helped make this book become a reality.

Thanks are due as always to the dynamic duo of Tim and Garry at Law Brief Publishing for agreeing to publish a second tome of mine. Their guidance and encouragement have been invaluable in getting this book out of my head and onto paper.

To my darling children, Luke and Joshua, for having a seemingly relentless belief that a second book was capable of being written and published by their Mother in between school runs, work, family time and Mum's taxi runs to their after school clubs. Your encouragement (even when in the form of "Are you not done yet? Mummy, hurry up and get it finished!") was welcomed more than you will ever know. I'm very blessed to have you both.

Last but by no means least, to Derek, my parents and mother-in-law for keeping my children entertained so I could put pen to paper to create this book.

CONTENTS

CHAPTER ONE

PRELIMINARY MATTERS

It is a sad fact of life that to deal with the administration of an estate, there has to be a death. If my 17 years or so experience in law has taught me anything, grief will affect people in a variety of ways. Some people become uber efficient and want the estate dealt with immediately so they can obtain closure on the experience. Other people will put off dealing with the administration of an estate until circumstances force them to accept the person has died and deal with the assets (or the debts as the case may be). Occasionally you find the estate administration had been put off that long, the person entitled to deal with the estate has also died, and you have not one but two (and in some cases more!) estates to deal with to get the assets to the right place. Some people will cry their way through the experience while others may appear flippant, angry or just downright rude. As an estate administrator, you will have to deal with every emotion a person has, and compared to any other area of law, you need to have compassion for what people are going through, particularly when their behaviour may not be that of a normal client. If you are not a "people person", this is not going to be the area of law for you.

Who is your client?

When dealing with a death, your client is usually the Personal Representative/Executor.

For testate estates (where there is a Will), this will (usually) be the person(s)/organisation(s) named as Executor in the Will or Codicil.

For intestate estates (where there is no Will), this will be the person or persons entitled to be appointed as the Personal Representative (see later in the book for the rules).

In some cases, the person who comes to you to advise you of the death may expect to be the personal Representative. With intestate estates, it is always best to have a genealogist check the family tree that has been provided to ensure you are instructed by the person with title to act. A list (which is by no means exclusive) of genealogists has been provided at the back of this book under "Useful Addresses". All of them offer family tree checking services. If you are going to put together a family tree for checking, try and collect as much information as you can regarding names, dates of birth, adoption, marriage, death and divorce and last known areas of residence of family members and the deceased.

Beneficiaries will often believe they are the client. They are not unless they are also the Executor/Personal Representative or they have instructed you directly as a beneficiary to deal with some aspect of the estate where the Executor has fallen short or as a disappointed heir. Where a beneficiary is also an Executor, ensure that you make clear to them that you are advising them in their capacity as Executor in connection with the administration of the estate and not as a beneficiary.

Managing Expectations

Once your client has been identified, you need to manage the expectations of the time it will take to wind up an estate. Given the current delays within the Probate Service[1] which can mean it is 5-6 months if not longer to obtain the Grant, as a minimum, clients and beneficiaries should be advised that they will not receive any funds for 6 months or so after the death. In reality, it is more likely to take around a year from instruction to investigate an estate, obtain Probate, ingather funds and wind up an estate and clients should be advised accordingly. This timeframe can be extended if you have overseas assets, properties to be sold, businesses to be sold, where Inheritance Tax is due and the District Valuer becomes involved or where the Department of Work and Pensions launches an investigation into whether all assets were declared when any benefits claims were made during life.

---

[1]   As at December 2022 based on the writer's current experience of obtaining Probate during 2022.

Terms of Engagement

It goes without saying that your client should receive terms of engagement. Estates are however tricky matters and what looks like a solvent estate on the initial meeting can quickly become insolvent as investigations into the extent of the estate get underway. Where this happens, it can often put full recovery of your fees in peril. Accordingly, consideration should be given as to whether your terms of engagement should include provision that in the event of insolvency the responsibility for paying fees should fall on the instructing party. Likewise, consider providing for the situation where the estate is solvent at the point of date of death but there are insufficient free proceeds to cover your fees or where it transpires the person originally instructing you does not have the title to act as Executor e.g. due to a later Will being discovered or a family member closer to the deceased in the intestate succession line being found.

Another point to consider is how you record time against your file. If you do not have an all singing, all dancing time electronic recording system that can capture all time spent on your file, you may wish to consider the use of an independent law accountant to assess your fees. In this event, provision should be built into your terms of engagement to enable you to do so and for the law accountant's fee to be an authorised expense of the administration of the estate.

In addition, you may wish to consider whether you want to include a risk commission in your terms of engagement which includes an uplift in fees based on the value of the assets ingathered, for example, Banks and Building Societies balances 0.75%, insurance policies 1% etc.

Reporting a Death

Sometimes, you may find out about the death through a hospital or the police. This may be because the deceased was in hospital prior to their death and advised who to contact in the event of their death. It can also be because the police have found the body in the house and have searched the house and found a Will or correspondence with your details on it. Depending on who is appointed as Executor or what family members are available, you may also have to register the death.

If the person has died in England and Wales, the death needs to be registered within 5 days. You can register the death if you:

    a.   are a relative;

    b.   were there at the time of death;

    c.   are the person who found the body;

    d.   are in the person in charge of a body;

    e.   are an administrator from the hospital (if the person died in hospital); or

    f.   are in charge of making funeral arrangements

You will need details of the deceased's:

1. Name

2. Maiden surname (if applicable)

3. Marital status

4. Date of birth

5. Date of death

6. Occupation

7. Last known address

8. Parents names and occupations

You will also need the causes of the death which should be provided to you in the form of a medical certificate from the doctor certifying the death.

You may also need the deceased's national insurance number and proof of the above such as their passport, driving licence, a bill showing their address, birth, marriage or adoption certificates.

> TIP – Do not make the mistake of starting to make arrangements for the funeral before the death is registered (for example in circumstances where your firm or partners thereof are named as Executor) otherwise you will find yourself in the hot seat for registering the death.
>
> TIP – If the deceased died in hospital without relatives being notified, try where possible to have the hospital register the death. You can thereafter obtain copies of the death certificate once it has been registered.

Extraordinary Registrations of Deaths

Scotland

You need to register the death within 8 days in Scotland including bank holidays and weekends. You will usually register the death at the Register of Births, Deaths and Marriages nearest to where the deceased died. As a consequence of the Covid-19 pandemic, this procedure has moved online to minimise contact[2]. Any person can register a death in Scotland as long as they can produce the correct documents although it is preferable that one of the following do so:

1. Any relative of the deceased;

2. Any person present when the person died;

3. The Executor or other legal representative;

4. Solicitor of the person who has died;

5. A person who lived with the deceased if they died at home; or

6. The funeral director and have permission from the family to register the death.

---

[2]   https://www.nrscotland.gov.uk/files//registration/scotlands-census-2021-registration-guidance-for-covid-19.pdf provides a flow chart for the process

Northern Ireland

The death is registered via the District Registration Office and needs to be completed within 5 days. You can register the death if you:

1. are a relative;

2. were there at the time of death;

3. are the person who found the body;

4. are in the person in charge of a body;

5. are an administrator from the hospital (if the person died in hospital);

6. are in charge of making funeral arrangements;

7. the governor, matron or chief officer of a public building where the death occurred; or

8. a person living in and responsible for a house, lodgings or apartments where the death occurred;

Foreign Deaths

If the person died abroad, you must register the death according to the regulations of the country in which the person died. It is also possible to register the death in the United Kingdom in addition to the country of death but it is not necessary to do so. If the death is also registered in the UK, this will enable a Consular death certificate to be obtained and evidence of the death will readily be available through the General Register Office[3] or in Scotland, the National Records Office of Scotland[4].

---

[3] https://www.gov.uk/general-register-office

[4] https://www.nrscotland.gov.uk/research or https://www.scotlandspeople.gov.uk/

If the person died on a foreign ship or aircraft, you must register the death in the country the ship or aircraft is registered in.

Funeral Arrangements and the right to dispose of a body

More often than not, the funeral will have been held or at the least instructed before the client comes to you to commence the administration of the estate. Your job in that case will simply be to ensure that the funeral is paid in the correct order of debts and transactions to be undertaken from the estate.

In most cases, there will be no argument over who makes the arrangements and it will simply be a case of "job done". However, there can be instances where the figurative "all hell breaks loose" over how the disposal of the deceased's body is to be arranged. In these cases, it is the Personal Representatives of the deceased who have title to determine how and where the body is disposed of[5]. If there are no Personal Representatives e,g. the deceased died intestate or where Probate hasn't been granted (and let's face it, in the vast majority of situations, Probate is unlikely to be granted before a funeral is capable of taking place!), then the person with the closest relationship to the deceased who could be appointed as administrator of the estate on intestacy[6] or who is named as Executor in the Will has the title to deal with the body[7]. Where there are two or more people who are in the same degree of relationship to the deceased for these purposes but cannot agree on how to dispose of the body, the body's disposal will be determined by the court.

---

[5] Ibuna & Another V Arroyo & Another [2012] EWHC 428 (Ch) provides an excellent commentary on this issue as well as observations on cross jurisdictional disputes over the disposal of a body.

[6] Buchanan V Milton [1999] 2 FLR 844

[7] Sharp V Lush (1879) 10 ChD 472

<u>TIP</u> – when writing Wills for clients and including provision for funeral instructions within the Will, ensure you advise your clients to tell their nearest and dearest their wishes for burial or cremation. It would not be the first time that a solicitor is notified about the death after the funeral has taken place only to discover on reading the Will that the deceased wished to be buried and had been cremated by the family. Needless to say, that situation can cause upset for the deceased's loved ones and there is really not a lot that you can do to rectify that situation after the fact!

CHAPTER TWO

INTESTATE ESTATES

An intestate estate occurs when a person dies without leaving a valid Will.

According to research, around 6 out of 10 adults in the UK don't have a Will[8]. Business development opportunities on the Will writing front aside, this means that more likely than not, you are going to have to administer an intestate estate at some point in your career.

Who will inherit when a person dies intestate in England and Wales will depend on the date of death.

Deaths from 1 October 2014 onwards

Where the deceased died on or after 1 October 2014, the following order of who can inherit will apply[9]:

1. Where the deceased was married/in a civil partnership, but has no surviving children (or remoter issue of a predeceasing child), then the estate passes in full on trust to the surviving spouse or civil partner;

2. Where the deceased leaves children (or representation by remoter descendants in the case of a predeceasing child) and also leaves a surviving spouse/civil partner, the distribution of the estate is as follows:-

   a. To the surviving spouse or civil partner:

---

[8]   See www.unbiased.co.uk's 2015 article " UK's will-writing 'black holes' revealed by research for unbiased.co.uk's Write A Will Week"

[9]   S46 Administration of Estates Act 1925 as amended by the Inheritance and Trustee Powers Act 2014

     i. All personal chattels of the deceased[10] without monetary limit;

     ii. A fixed net sum (currently £270,000[11]) free of death duties and costs together with simple interest on it from the date of death until the legacy is satisfied with interest thereon at the Bank of England rate that had effect at the end of the day on which the deceased died;

     iii. One half share of the residue of the estate – that is to say everything that is left over after settlement of all debts, funeral expenses, taxes, legacies and administration expenses – on trust

   b. To the children (or remoter descendants of predeceasing children)

     i. one half share of the residue of the estate on statutory trust;

3. Where there are children but no spouse/civil partner of the deceased then the entire estate passes equally between the children of the deceased (with representation by issue in the case of a predeceasing child);

4. In the event that the deceased was not survived by a spouse, children or remoter issue, then if one or both of the deceased's parents are still alive, the entire estate passes equally between the parents or to the survivor of them as the case may be;

5. In the event that the deceased was not survived by a spouse, children or remoter issue, or parents, then the entire estate passes

---

[10] S55 (1) (X) Administration of Estates Act 1925

[11] At December 2022 – The Administration of Estates Act 1925 (Fixed Net Sum) Order 2020. The specified sum was £250,000 for deaths which occurred between 1st October 2014 and 6th February 2020.

equally between their siblings (with representation by issue in the case of a predeceasing sibling). For these purposes, siblings are defined as siblings of the full blood (in simple terms, where the deceased and the siblings share the same Mother and Father);

6. In the event that the deceased was not survived by a spouse, children or remoter issue, parents or full blood siblings, then the estate passes equally between the half siblings with representation by issue in the case of a predeceasing half sibling (A half sibling for these purposes is a sibling who shares a single parent with the deceased);

7. In the event that the deceased was not survived by a spouse, children or remoter issue, parents or full or half-blood siblings, the entire estate passes equally between and to the survivor of the deceased's grandparents. This provision includes both maternal and paternal grandparents ie if the deceased was survived by both sets of grandparents, each grandparent would receive a quarter share of the estate;

8. In the event that the deceased was not survived by a spouse, children or remoter issue, parents, full or half-blood siblings or grandparents, the entire estate passes equally between aunts and uncles of the full blood of the deceased (both maternal and paternal) (with representation by issue in the event of a predeceasing aunt or uncle);

9. In the event that the deceased was not survived by a spouse, children or remoter issue, parents, full or half-blood siblings, grandparents and aunts and uncles of the full blood, then the estate passes equally between the half aunts and uncles with representation by issue in the case of a predeceasing half aunt or uncle;

10. In the event that the deceased is survived by none of the foregoing relatives, the estate passes to the Crown or to the Duchy of

Lancaster or to the Duke of Cornwall for the time being, as the case may be, as *bona vacantia*[12].

For these purposes, the family history only goes back as far as grandparents on both maternal and paternal sides but can descend from there through as many generations as is required to find a living heir.

Deaths prior to 1 October 2014

For deaths which occurred before 1st October 2014, a different set of rules applied in connection with the provision for a surviving spouse/civil partner and children as follows:

1. Where the deceased was married/in a civil partnership, but has no surviving children (or remoter issue of a predeceasing child), then the estate passes in full to the surviving spouse or civil partner;

2. Where the deceased left children (with representation by issue in the case of predeceasing children) but no surviving spouse/civil partner, then the estate passes in full to the children (or their issue as the case may be) equally between and to the survivor of them;

3. Where the deceased left children (or representation by remoter descendants in the case of a predeceasing child) and also leaves a surviving spouse/civil partner, the distribution of the estate was as follows:-

    a. To the surviving spouse or civil partner:

        i. All personal chattels of the deceased[13] without monetary limit;

---

[12] See www.gov.uk/unclaimed-estates-bona-vacantia for details on how to report an estate that appears to be heirless

[13] S55 (1) (X) Administration of Estates Act 1925

      ii. A statutory gift[14] plus interest running from the date of death to the date the gift is satisfied;

      iii. One half share of the residue of the estate – that is to say everything that is left over after settlement of all debts, funeral expenses, taxes, legacies and administration expenses – on life interest trust with the option to elect to convert the trust to a capital sum (particularly useful in small estates)[15];

  b. To the children (or remoter descendants of predeceasing children)

      i. one half share of the residue of the estate on statutory trust equally among them if more than one and contingent upon the earlier of them attaining the age of 18 years old or marrying (including entering a civil partnership); and

      ii. the remainder of the spousal life interest trust on the spouse's death.

4. Where the deceased was survived by a spouse/civil partner, parents and siblings of the full blood (with representation by issue of predeceasing siblings) but had no children or remoter descendants the distribution of the estate was as follows:-

  a. To the surviving spouse or civil partner:

      i. All personal chattels of the deceased[16] without monetary limit;

---

[14] £125,000 for deaths prior to 1 February 2009. £250,000 for deaths post 1 February 2009 but before 1 October 2014.

[15] S47A(1) Administration of Estates Act 1925 which no longer applies post 1 October 2014

[16] S55 (1) (X) Administration of Estates Act 1925

      ii. A statutory gift[17] plus interest running from the date of death to the date the gift is satisfied;

  iii. One half share of the residue of the estate absolutely.

  b. Where the deceased is survived by parents:

      i. The parents will take the remainder of the residue equally between them or in full to the survivor of them absolutely;

  c. Where the deceased is survived by siblings (with representation by issue of predeceasing siblings) but not by parents:

      i. The siblings (with representation by issue) will take the remainder of the residue equally between them or in full to the survivor of them absolutely;

5. Where there is no spouse/civil partner and no children (including representation by issue) then the order of succession is as follows:

6. To the parents of the deceased equally among them and to the survivor;

7. To siblings of the full blood (with representation by issue) equally among them and to the survivor or survivors of them;

8. To siblings of the half-blood (with representation by issue) equally among them and to the survivor or survivors of them;

9. To grandparents equally among them and to the survivor or survivors of them;

---

17 £200,000 for deaths prior to 1 February 2009. £450,000 for deaths post 1 February 2009 but before 1 October 2014.

10. To aunts and uncles of the whole blood (with representation by issue) equally among them and to the survivor or survivors of them;

11. To aunts and uncles of the half-blood (with representation by issue) equally among them and to the survivor or survivors of them;

12. In the event that the deceased is survived by none of the foregoing relatives, the estate passes to the Crown or to the Duchy of Lancaster or to the Duke of Cornwall for the time being, as the case may be, as *bona vacantia*.

Children

It should be noted that there is no distinction in terms of succession rules following the death of a parent as to whether the child is legitimate (born to parents who are married) or illegitimate (born to parents who are not married). Likewise, once a child is adopted, the line of succession switches from that of their biological parents to that of their adopted parents and they are treated as if they were a biological child of their adoptive parents.

The only distinction which applies relates to succession to an illegitimate child's estate. Where the father is not named on the birth certificate, the father and all of the father's relatives are deemed to have predeceased the child[18].

Where IVF is involved, the woman carrying the child is deemed to be the mother of the child for succession purposes notwithstanding that she may have no genetic connection to the child[19]. Likewise, the husband of the woman carrying the child is deemed to be the father for succession purposes (again notwithstanding that he may not have a biological connection to the child). There is however an exception to this, namely

---

[18] S18(2) Family Law Reform Act 1987 as amended by the Inheritance and Trustees Powers Act 2014.

[19] S27 Family Law Reform Act 1987

in circumstances where the husband did not consent to the implantation of the embryo[20]. Succession away from the carrier and her spouse/civil partner will only happen once the baby is formally adopted by its "new" parents (for example, where a surrogate carrier is used).

Cohabiting Partners

You will notice the complete absence of any mention of cohabiting partners on intestacy. This is because there are no automatic rights of succession for cohabiting partners. A claim can however be made for provision for a surviving cohabitant under the Inheritance (Provision for Family and Dependants) Act 1975 (more of which later).

Spouse/Civil Partners dying in quick succession

It is important to note that where:

1. The death occurs after 1 January 1996; and

2. The surviving spouse/civil partner of the deceased survives the deceased **but** dies within 28 days of the deceased;

Then the now deceased surviving spouse/civil partner is treated as having predeceased the deceased and the estate of the now deceased surviving spouse/civil partner not be entitled to receive anything from the estate of the first spouse/civil partner to die[21].

Where the death occurred prior to 1 January 1996, the estate is dealt with as if there had never been a spouse or civil partner.

---

[20] S1 Legitimacy Act 1976 as amended by S28 Family Law Reform Act 1987

[21] S46 (2A) Administration of Estates Act 1925

Partial Intestacies

This is a situation which arises in a testate estate but a defect occurs as follows:

1. The deceased has failed to dispose of his full estate (commonly happens in DIY Wills where the testator thinks they have to narrate who gets each specific asset and they either forget about an asset or fail to review their Will, change assets (e.g. purchases a new house) and forget to update their Will; or

2. Where there is no destination over in the situation where a named beneficiary predeceases or fails to comply with contingent conditions of inheritance (e.g. dying prior to attaining a certain age);

In these cases, there is a hybrid model of succession deployed whereby the Will covers what it can including Executor appointments and the rest of the estate not otherwise dealt with through the Will is dealt with according to the intestacy rules detailed above.

CHAPTER THREE

TESTATE ESTATES

A testate Estate is one in which there is a valid Will. A Will will normally appoint Executors, provide details of any legacies and deal with the division of the residue of the estate. It may on occasion provide details of the manner in which the body should be disposed of and provide guardians for minor children as well as any specific powers of the Executors.

You may also have one or more Codicils to the Will to contend with. A Codicil to the Will is a document amending the terms of a Will or a previous Codicil.

Locating the Will (and any Codicils)

The first stage in a testate estate is to locate the Will and any Codicils.

The Will (and any Codicils) will normally be held by the solicitor who drafted the Will. In this situation, most people will have a letter from their solicitor with a copy of the Will among their personal papers that will lead you to the firm that holds the Will. This may lead you into a little bit of a detective work if the firm in question no longer exists or has been taken over multiple times.

Of course, a solicitor is not required to make a Will. If the whereabouts of a non-solicitor Will is not immediately apparent, a thorough search of the deceased's property should be undertaken to ascertain if the Will is in the house or otherwise located elsewhere.

It also used to be common practise for Banks to provide will writing and storage facilitates. It is therefore worth asking the deceased's Bank if they hold anything in storage for the deceased. If there is nothing in storage with the Bank, the Bank will also be provide details of which law firms either provided their will writing services or to whom their business was outsourced too on closure of the Bank's in house will writing department.

If a person has had a conversation with the now deceased testator in which they advised that they had made a Will but did not disclose who with, if you know the approximate geographical area of where the deceased would have been at the time the purported Will was made, you can write to the solicitors in that area to enquire if they held a Will (this is where your admin assistant with mail merge skills will become your new best friend!). Depending on the area and popularity of law firm businesses, this may be involve a handful of letters or may involve several hundred if a major city is involved. The costs involved in conducting such a search should be weighed up against the potential for a disappointed beneficiary who may be excluded from benefiting in the event that a Will cannot be located.

You may also wish to check with the Certainty Will Register[22] to ascertain if they hold details of the Will. The Certainty Will Register doesn't hold the actual Will but holds details of where a Will is held. It is supposed to act like a central register of Wills so that Wills can be found and enacted with ease.

Lastly, it is also possible for Wills to be lodged with the safe keeping facility within the Probate Registry. Contact the London Probate Registry to ascertain if they have a Will stored with them.

<u>Validity of Will</u>

Once the Will has been located, in order to be a self-proving valid Will that can be admitted into the Probate process, the testamentary document needs to meet the following criteria:

1. Have a designated testator – that is to say, the person making the Will;

2. The testator must have been aged 18 years old or over[23] when the Will was granted;

---

[22] www.nationalwillregister.co.uk

[23] S 7 Wills Act 1837 as amended by S3(1) Family Law Reform Act 1969

3. The testator must have had mental capacity to enter into the Will[24];

4. The Will must (usually[25]) be in writing (either handwritten or typed)[26] although the medium upon which it is written can vary[27];

5. The testator must know of and approve the contents of the Will;

6. The testator must have signed the Will[28] (or in circumstances where the testator is unable to sign e.g. he is blind, have the Will signed on his behalf in his presence and at his direction) in the presence of two independent witnesses who are not named in the Will, not married to anyone named in the Will at the time of execution of the Will[29] and who are also over the age of 18 and

---

[24] Banks v. Goodfellow 1870. LR 5 QB 549

[25] S11 Wills Act 1837 and S2 Wills (Soldiers and Sailors) Act 1918 provides the mechanism for persons under the age of 18 years old to create a Will where they are serving in the armed forces or merchant navy. In these circumstances, the Will does not need to be in writing and can be made orally – see In the Estate of W C Yates (1919) P 93. This is known as a privileged Will.

[26] Watch out for documents drafted in both pencil and ink. There is a rebuttable presumption that in this scenario, the words in pencil are deemed to be deliberative only and will be excluded from Probate. See In the Goods of Adams (1872) 2 P & D 367. Stick to preparing Wills 100% in ink would be my advice!

[27] Hudson V Barnes [1926] 43 TLR 7 which dealt with an eggshell Will (the mind boggles!). Safe to say, a Will produced on regular paper with ink of some description is by far the preferable and safest method!

[28] Traditionally this is on the last page after all of the provisions of the Will but may be elsewhere – see Wood V Smith [1993] Ch 90 for commentary.

[29] S15 Wills Act 1837 provides that where a witness is named in the Will as a beneficiary or where their spouse or civil partner is named as a beneficiary in the Will, that beneficiary will forfeit their entitlement under the Will. This can be gotten around in circumstances where there is a later Codicil executed which does not contain a conflict of interests upon execution as

the witnesses must also have signed the Will at the Testator's request and in the Testator's presence.

<u>Keeping the Will safe</u>

It goes without saying that you need to keep the Will safe to administer the estate as it will be required to obtain Probate to the estate. It should be kept in the strong room at your firm. Ideally when sending a principal Will anywhere, it should be sent by some form of tracked delivery in order that should it go missing, you can establish in Court at what point it went missing, who the carrier was and who was the last person to have it.

If using Royal Mail, their recorded delivery service simply provides a signature upon receipt (and in these post Covid 19 days, it doesn't necessarily follow that the signature obtained will be that of the recipient. It may well be that of the delivering Postie which is used). If you need to track the full journey of the document (and where principal Wills are concerned, I would want to), their Special Delivery should be used as it tracks the entire journey from collection to delivery.

Hays DX also provide both regular and tracked delivery options as do many of the other carriers such as Fedex, DHL etc

---

the Codicil will be deemed to have republished the Will effectively washing away the conflict.

CHAPTER FOUR

COMMORIENTES RULE

There may be circumstances in which it is unclear who survived who in a spouse/civil partner couple, for example, where the couple are both involved in a fatal accident and have died before the emergency services reach them. This can obviously have a significant impact on the devolution of the estate assets.

The Commorientes rule deals with this scenario and is governed by s 184 Law of Property Act 1925. It provides that the elder of the married/civil partnership couple will be presumed to have died first. This assumption can however be rebutted in circumstances where:

1. There is a court order to the contrary; or

2. Where the elder of the couple died intestate, in which case the younger person of the couple will be presumed to have died first.

CHAPTER FIVE

COMMENCING THE ADMINISTRATION OF THE ESTATE

In order to administer the estate, you will need as a bare minimum a full extract death certificate for the deceased. On registration of the death, It will be necessary to pay to obtain at least one full extract. Where it is a large estate or where there are multiple life policies, it would be wise to obtain a couple of copies of the full death certificate to speed up the circulation of documents to asset holders.

If no full extract death certificate was obtained or if further copies are required, these can be ordered online through the General Register Office[30].

Where it is a testate estate, you will also need the original Will and any Codicils and informal writings.

Other documents concerning the deceased which would be useful to have include:

1. Birth certificate

2. Adoption certificate

3. Marriage certificate

4. Separation agreement

5. Decrees of Divorce

---

[30] www.gov.uk/order-copy-birth-marriage-death-certificate

6. Passport

7. Driving licence

8. HMRC statement (which may not be available if the deceased had not previously been in the self-assessment regime)

9. Statement of benefits letter from the Department of Work and Pensions

10. National insurance number

Thereafter, you need to ascertain the extent of the estate. That means locating all of the deceased's assets and ascertaining the extent of their debts.

Why do you need to locate the assets?

The Personal Representatives will need to compile an inventory of the assets and debts of the deceased to ascertain:

1. whether there is Inheritance Tax due on the estate; and

2. that all debts have been settled and all assets have been identified for distribution to the beneficiaries

Given that a declaration is required to be given by the Personal Representatives both on applying for Probate/Letters of Administration and on the Inheritance Tax forms confirming that the details contained in the documents are correct to the best of their knowledge, it is important that the extent of the assets and debts are ascertained in order to calculate the amount of Inheritance Tax due (if any) on the estate and ensure that the Personal Representatives make as truthful a declaration on the extent of the estate assets.

Finding assets and debts

If you are lucky, the deceased will have been super organised and you will be able to collect their box of papers with details of all their assets from the bottom of their wardrobe or other safe place. More likely than not, you are going to have to get your detective cap on and go digging to ascertain the extent of the assets and debts.

It used to be the case that you could put a 6-12 months redirection of mail on the deceased's residence and you could be reasonably certain you would have caught all potential assets and debts. While a mail redirection should still be organised where the property is now unoccupied, as more and more people manage their banking and investments online, it is becoming increasingly difficult to locate assets and debts where there is not a paper trail.

Paper documents will always be your starting point. If you are tasked with trying to find papers, you will need to search the property from head to toe. You may wish to consider whether a colleague should accompany you in case any money is found. Before you take any offence, I am not considering any skulduggery on your part by suggesting you take a colleague with you! This is simply to cover you in the event a family member or friend suggests there was cash or other valuables in the property and you either can't find them or don't find as much as expected and you are then in the hot seat as prime suspect no 1! It also covers you in the hopefully unlikely event that you were to be mugged en route to your firm's bank with cash from the property as there will be a witness to the incident.

People stash details of their assets (and indeed their cash!) in the most unlikely of places so on a house visit search everywhere… and I mean everywhere! The usual suspect places for cash and assets are wardrobes, drawers, under beds and desks. Coat pockets and bags are also a likely source of bank cards and cash. Some of the more unusual places where I have found documents and cash are in the freezer, the biscuit tin, in pots in the cupboard, behind paintings and in the cistern! (I wish I could take credit for the genius of looking in the cistern but alas, it was a house clearing company that I had booked to attend who suggested it as a place they had found cash previously and lo and behold we found some in a plastic bag taped to the inside of the lid!). Under floorboards is another place to look – now I am not suggesting you rip up every floorboard in sight on the off chance that you find a secret stash but if you find yourself walking across a particularly squeaky board near the edge of a carpet, it may just be worthwhile having a peek.

Look in wallets and purses to find membership, loyalty scheme and bank cards. Unused gift cards can also have a value in an estate.

Things to look out for when searching a house

In addition to looking for details of assets and debts, there are some other things that you should look out for to secure the deceased's estate.

Passport

Not strictly speaking an asset but should you come across passports for the deceased – expired or current – these should be sent to the Passport Office for cancellation. You should ask the family whether these should be returned as the Passport Office is happy to do so but will destroy them if not otherwise instructed. The reason for cancellation of passports is to prevent identity theft. You should also keep a copy of the passport in your file in case you need to provide proof of signature of the deceased to link assets to them[31].

Driving licence

Much like passports, notifying the DVLA about the death isn't about finding assets as such but about prevention of identity theft. You should however ask them to check if there are any vehicles registered in the deceased's name that you have not otherwise found out about.

---

[31] For example, National Savings and Investments will often ask for a specimen signature if they receive a speculative enquiry concerning premium bonds and are attempting to match up bonds registered as held at a previous address of the deceased.

Vehicles

You will need the V5 for any vehicles owned by the deceased before you can sell or transfer the vehicle. The logbook would also be useful to locate particularly if the vehicle is to be sold to obtain the highest possible price.

You can check the MOT history of the vehicle at www.gov.uk/check-mot-history and the vehicle tax history of the vehicle at www.gov.uk/get-vehicle-information-from-dvla and arrange MOT/vehicle tax or declare the vehicle as off road for vehicle tax as appropriate.

Bank/Credit Cards

When dealing with bank and credit cards, cut the cards in two or more pieces to ensure they cannot be used (preferably through the "chip" on the card and signature strip). This is particularly important now with the advent of contactless technologies to prevent them being used post death inappropriately, particularly if they are being posted back to the bank.

Honours

Receipt of Honours such as OBE, CBE, MBE etc are more common than you might expect. If you find an award among the deceased's personal effects or are otherwise told that they held an Honour, you will need to advise The Chancery at St James Palace. While I have yet to have a request from the Chancery to return an award, it is a question I usually ask on notification of the death to ensure the award ends up in the right place. I also normally ask if The Chancery has any additional obligations that the Executors need to comply with. The staff at The Chancery are extremely helpful at navigating you through what needs to be done.

Share Certificates

If you find share certificates (they do still exist even with the popularity of Discretionary Fund Managers!), take them back to the office with you and put in your safe until you can establish which ones are valid (assuming of course that your firm has the necessary permissions from the Law Society or are otherwise regulated by the Financial Conduct Authority to conduct incidental financial services business).

Insurance certificates

This can be for home insurance as well as life and/or accident insurance. Keep these safe as they may need to be produced to make a claim.

Investment Bonds

If you find original bond documents, keep these safe as you may need to produce them to sell or transfer the asset.

Secure valuables

If there are any valuables in the property such as jewellery, you may wish to take these back to the office to put in your safe or where they are to be sold, consider consigning them to an auction house for safe keeping.

Property

While title deeds can likely be found with a mortgage provider or a solicitor, sometime they can be located within the property so it is worthwhile looking to see if you can find them or otherwise details of who may hold them so you can obtain them during the administration of the estate. Of particular concern are locating titles to unregistered land. While fairly uncommon, reconstituting title deeds to prove title to unregistered land can be a fairly lengthy and expensive process and therefore the sooner a search commences the better.

Changing the locks

You may wish to consider whether you wish to change the locks to the property particularly where the property is unoccupied following the death or where there is a family fall out over who is getting what from the house.

CHAPTER SIX

PROTECTING THE EXECUTORS

There are certain steps which can be taken to protect the Personal Representatives against claims in the estate.

S27 Trustee Act 1925 adverts

As soon as possible after being instructed, S27 Trustee Act 1925 adverts should be placed in the London Gazette and where the deceased owned land or a business, a newspaper local to where the land or business was situated.

Where the deceased died testate, the adverts can be placed as soon as the death occurs by the Executors.

Where the deceased died intestate, the adverts can only be placed once Letters of Administration have been granted. This is because the Personal Representatives power stems from the Grant whereas for testate estates the power to act stems from the Will and any Codicils.

The adverts enable any unknown creditors or beneficiaries to makes themselves known to the Personal representatives. The adverts have a cessation date of 2 months after they go to print. While the 2-month window is in force, the personal representatives should not distribute the estate. If they choose to distribute during that period and a creditor presents themselves then the personal representatives will be personally liable to meet the extent of the debt – needless to say, a position that no one wishes to find themselves in!

Once the adverts have expired, the personal representatives can distribute the estate.

A number of companies offer the placing of these adverts[32].

Inheritance (Provision For Family And Dependants) Act 1975

You will probably know fairly quickly after being instructed if there is a family member who is unhappy about the distribution of the estate and therefore that a claim arising under the above legislation is likely to follow. Where a claim is intimated, distribution of the estate should not occur until directions from the Court are received.

However, in some cases, a claimant may not immediately make themselves known. If there are rumblings within the family that someone is unhappy but no formal intimation has been made or where intimation has been made but no further action has been taken by the potential claimant to progress their claim, distribution should be withheld until 6 months have elapsed after the Grant has been made otherwise the Executors can find themselves personally responsible for meeting a successful claim. It should be noted that the placing and expiry of S27 Trustee Act 1925 adverts will not get around the 6-month period stated above.

---

[32] I normally use https://www.legalads.co.uk/trustee-act-form.php as they can place both London Gazette and local adverts in a single instruction however there are other providers. Your firm may have a specific agency that they use for their local area.

CHAPTER SEVEN

INITIAL INVESTIGATIONS

Once you believe you have located all of the information concerning the deceased's possible assets and debts and secured any vehicles and property, you need to commence with the initial investigations.

Depending on the nature of the possible assets and debts and how quick asset holders respond, this stage is likely to take around 12-16 weeks to complete. This timeframe is likely to be significantly extended if you have foreign assets that need to be identified or if there is a business involved.

You will need to contact every potential asset holder and creditor to assess the extent of the asset/debt at the date of death. The assessment should always be on the basis of an open market valuation between a willing buyer and seller. Unlike insurance valuations, the valuation is undertaken on the price that a willing buyer would be prepared to buy the asset in its current condition rather than on a new for old valuation basis.

Property and land

Where the estate is not subject to Inheritance Tax, an estimated value for property and/or land can be used for Probate purposes. This could be from an estate agent or from an online portal which provides estimates of house prices[33].

Where the estate is likely or going to be subject to Inheritance Tax or in circumstances where the market is on a rapid upward trajectory and Capital Gains Tax on disposal is likely to be an issue, you should obtain a formal valuation of the property and/or land from a surveyor. When instructing the survey, you need to advise that it is a survey for Inheritance Tax purposes and that it should be for an open market value on the date of death between a willing buyer and seller. You also need to

---

[33] See for example, https://www.zoopla.co.uk/house-prices/

advise them to take account of any development potential for the property and/or land as this is also subject to Inheritance Tax. You might also wish to ask the surveyor for a reinstatement valuation for insurance purposes to make sure your Personal Representatives have sufficiently insured the building in the event that a claim requires to be made.

If there is any disagreement between the Personal Representatives, beneficiaries or indeed your own professional view on the figure which is returned from the valuer, you may wish to consider instructing a second valuation on the same terms to corroborate the value provided. If nothing else, your Personal Representatives will be able to demonstrate that they have taken all reasonable steps to verify the value of the property in the event of a query from the District Valuer. Of course, this could lead to the situation whereby the valuers disagree on the value to be used. Where the values differ significantly, you may need to instruct a third valuation to identify and set aside the errant value. In any event, your surveyor should be able to discuss with you their reasoning for the value they have attributed to your property.

Personal Effects

For Inheritance Tax purposes, personal effects are valued on an old for old basis. Essentially, what this means is what a willing buyer would be prepared to pay for the items in their current condition in open market conditions. This is different to an insurance valuation which would provide cover for a new replacement.

For a significant part of the population, the deceased will only have what can be deemed as regular personal effects, for example, beds, wardrobes, sofas, pots and pans etc. Many household items will no longer meet current health and safety standards and will therefore be unsellable and attract a nil value for these purposes.

Again, if Inheritance Tax is likely or going to be an issue, you should have the contents professionally valued. Most auction houses offer this service. The valuation should be stated to be assessed as at the date of death. It is not uncommon for a nil or nominal value to be attributed to the value of the personal effects by a valuer where the deceased had only what might be deemed to be regular household contents, particularly for properties which have been in need of substantial modernisation where the contents do not meet current fire retardancy standards.

You will also wish to consider whether personal effects should be formally valued if there are potential Inheritance (Provision for Family and Dependants) Act 1975 claims on the estate. If using an estimated valuation, you should advise the claimants that an estimated value has been used to minimise costs to the estate and that they are able to request a formal valuation to confirm the final value used. If a valuation is requested, it goes without saying that the claimant may receive more or less than they would have done with the estimated valuation.

If the deceased had any collections such as stamps, coins, crystal, Wedgewood plates etc, these should be valued by an appropriate valuer. If an auction house is unable to value them for whatever reason, they should be able to provide you with details of appropriate valuers.

Vehicles

You can use either a valuation for the vehicle such as from Parkers[34] or Glass[35] or you can use a sold valuation if the car is sold between the death and obtaining Probate (assuming the sold price is representative of the value that would have been obtained at the date of death).

If you cannot locate the V5 for any vehicles owned by the deceased, you will need to contact the DVLA for a replacement before the vehicle can be sold or transferred. You will also need to check the MOT[36] and taxation status[37] of the vehicle to ensure that the vehicle does not get impounded for being illegal on either front.

---

[34] https://www.parkers.co.uk/

[35] https://glass.co.uk

[36] https://www.gov.uk/check-mot-status

[37] https://www.gov.uk/check-vehicle-tax

If the vehicle is being sole or transferred, you will need to apply for a refund of vehicle tax as it is no longer the case that the vehicle tax transfers with the ownership of the vehicle.

Registration Plate

Believe it or not, some registration plates for vehicles can have a value separate from the vehicle it is registered to which can run from a few hundred pounds to seven figures. The world's most expensive registration plate was held in Dubai and sold for an eye watering AED33m/GB£7.324m[38]. Registration marks which accrue value are usually private registration marks. A value can be obtained from a car or plate dealership.

Caravan

Caravans will vary in value and usually the caravan park upon which it is parked will be able to provide a resale value. One thing to bear in mind with caravans that are on a caravan park is that on site fees will continue to accrue. The estate may also be subject to winter storage charges and transfer of pitch charges going forward.

Yachts, Boats, Ships and Aircraft

Like a vehicle, boats and aircraft will need to be valued for Inheritance Tax purposes. This is not an exact science (much like cars) as the value will depend on how well they have been maintained. Contact a broker for a value who may well send out a surveyor to confirm the estimated value. As with any other asset, the true value of the asset will only be discovered when it is placed on the open market.

For the purposes of where the asset is placed on Inheritance Tax returns, the boat or aircraft will fall under the jurisdiction of the country in which it is registered

---

[38] Balwinder Sahni, an Indian Businessman based in Dubai purchased the plate in 2016.

One thing you will need to make sure you do is make arrangements to keep the boat berthed or the aircraft standing while the administration of the estate is undertaken. You may be able to negotiate payment of fees to be paid post Probate or where there are no funds in the estate, the Personal Representatives may need to make other financial arrangements to meet the costs (which may include a loan or a beneficiary taking over responsibility who can be reimbursed from the estate at a later date).

Bank/Building Society Accounts

You will need to ascertain the capital balance on the account and any interest accrued but not yet paid at the date of death.

With increasing use of paperless statements, you may need to rely on the bank/building society card to ascertain which bank or building society the deceased had accounts with. Not all cards will have an account number printed on them. If you haven't found statements in the house for the bank or building society and the card doesn't have an account number, I normally attach the cut-up cards to the initial letter with sticky tape to help the bank locate the deceased's accounts. This practice will soon be obsolete as the banks move over to online portal notifications systems. Details of some of the exisiting portals are at the useful addresses section of this book.

When contacting a bank for details of the assets, you should also ask them to provide details of any interest paid during the current and previous tax year in order that you can ascertain the extent of any tax that the deceased owed or was due to be refunded by HMRC.

In addition, you should ask for details of all standing orders and direct debits on the accounts. This will give you leads for other assets which you may not have found paperwork for (for example bank accounts or investments which are funded regularly by the deceased) as well details of who the deceased was indebted too and the basics like who supplies the utilities for the deceased.

You should also ask whether the bank or building society is holding anything in safe custody for the deceased. Banks frequently used to offer a safe custody service and you may find other assets or important papers in their vaults.

Business Interests

A business interest for the deceased will take the form of the deceased being a sole trader, being a partner in a partnership or owning shares in a company.

The starting point for valuing the business will be the deceased's accountant. Where the deceased has been a sole trader or a partner, it will be necessary for the books to be brought up to the date of date of death to establish the date of death value.

Unless a partnership deed provides otherwise, on the death of a partner, the partnership is dissolved and wound up with the net assets (or liabilities) shared between the partners and the deceased partner's estate in accordance with the Partnership Act.

Share in private companies

These are shares in traditionally family-owned companies and are not listed on a trading exchange. You will need to ascertain the type and number of shares that the deceased held. While Companies House can provide some information, you will not necessarily be able to establish all of the information you will need to proceed with Confirmation. You will therefore require the assistance of the Company Secretary if there is one and the company's accountant. You will also need to acquire three years of accounts for the company (or as many sets of accounts as are available where the company is less than 3 years old). The accountant for the company should be able to establish the value per share for the deceased's shares in the company which may be more or less than other shareholders depending on whether the deceased was either a majority or a minority shareholder in the company.

You should also check what the position is with the disposal of the shares for later on in the estate. Often private companies have limitations on who can acquire the shares, for example, a direction that the shares must be offered to other shareholders first before any transfer to an external party can be undertaken which can impact how the asset is administered by the Personal Representatives. Download the Memorandum and Articles of Association from Companies House[39] (as well as any updates) as soon as possible to ascertain if there any conflicts between the Will/intestate devolution of the estate and the operational requirements of the company.

<u>Shares in listed companies</u>

What is a listed company? A listed company is a public company whose shares are listed on a recognised stock exchange either in the UK or abroad. The most common exchanges in the UK are the London Stock Exchange (LSA) and the Alternative Investment Market (AIM).

While most companies have moved or are moving over to non-certificated holdings in electronic format i.e. you receive a statement detailing the number and type of shares held rather than accumulating individual share certificates, it is still possible to have certificated shares in listed companies. You will need to write to the Registrar[40] to ascertain the amount and type of shares held as at the date of death.

When trying to ascertain who the registrar for a company is, search online for the name of the company plus investor relations. That will normally bring up the details of the registrar if there is one or will otherwise provide contact details for the company itself if their register of shareholders is maintained in house.

Once you know the type and amount of shares held in each company, you will need to undertake what is known as a quarter up valuation which will be used to obtain Probate and calculate the Inheritance Tax due. In order to calculate the quarter up value, you will need the high and low values on the date of death (where the death was at the weekend, you can

---

[39] www.companieshouse.gov.uk

[40] Search online for the name of the company plus investor relations and it should bring up all of the shareholder information including who the registrar is. The main three registrars can be found in the useful addresses section of this book.

use the value on either the Friday before or the Monday after the death). Historic share values can be found on sites such as https://finance.yahoo.com/quote/yhoo/history/ or https://www.hl.co.uk /help/dealing/share-dealing/share-prices2/can-i-find-historic-share-prices

The quarter up calculation is as follows:

Step 1: High value - low value = X

Step 2: low value + (x/4) = price per share on date of death

You will also need to ascertain from the registrar if there are dividends which were declared on or before the death but which had not been paid at the date of death as these will also contribution to the gross estate for Inheritance Tax purposes. These are known as ex-dividends.

In addition, you should ask the registrars if there is any cash outstanding at the date of death such as uncashed dividends or dissentients funds (these are funds usually issued to shareholders where a company takeover has happened and the shareholder did not consent to the takeover but it happened regardless and they received cash in exchange for their shares).

Where you have found share certificates, you should ask the registrar to confirm the share certificates that are valid for the holding as you will need these should you have to sell or transfer the shares. It also gives you time to try and trace any missing share certificates before the point at which you need them post Probate. If you do not have all of the share certificates, the Personal Representatives will need to complete an indemnity for the missing share certificates to enable a new share certificate for the balance of the missing share certificates to be issued before the affected shares can be sold or transferred. An administration fee will usually need to be paid before the shares will be sold or transferred which you will be advised of by the Registrar.

You will also need details of the dividends declared in the tax year to date of death and the previous tax year to calculate whether there are sums due to or by HMRC to the estate.

Foreign Shares

In addition to the requirements for UK registered shareholdings above, it will be necessary to narrate a conversion rate from the local currency for Inheritance Tax purposes e.g. at a rate of Euro0.80 to GB£1. Sites such www.xe.com will let you work out the applicable currency conversion rate at the date of death.

Share Portfolio

Where the deceased held a portfolio of shares with a stockbroker, the broker will be able to provide you with a quarter up valuation of the assets held along with details of where the asset is situated, cash outstanding and ex-dividends.

National Savings & Investments

As with the assets above, you will need to ascertain the capital balance and any interest which has accrued to date of death. Products offered include premium bonds, bank accounts, ISAs and savings certificates[41].

Premium Bonds are a type of savings mechanism. Holders of Premium Bonds do not receive interest on their savings but receive an entry into a monthly prize draw for every £1 bond they hold. Prizes range from £25 to £1m every month. Savers can have a maximum of £50,000 invested in Premium Bonds at any one time. All prizes are free of Income Tax and Capital Gains Tax. Bonds can remain in the draw for up to 1 year after the death of the deceased. On the first anniversary, the bonds plus any prizes will be repaid (although early encashment is available if so desired by the Personal Representatives). Prizes won during the year following the death are also free of Income Tax and Capital Gains Tax.

Life Policies

Life policy companies will usually insist on seeing the original death certificate before they will determine what the claim amount is, if any.

---

[41] See www.nsandi.com for further information

You will need to check the letter they provide you with on notification of the death as the details of the final claim amount may well be different from the value as at date of death due to fluctuating investment elements (if applicable), final bonuses and interest. Particularly where Inheritance Tax is an issue, you do not wish to overstate the amount that it is due to the estate.

State Benefits

When writing to the Department for Work and Pensions, you will need to enquire about the type of benefits claimed by the deceased (including state pension), whether there are any sums due to or by the estate and obtain details of the beneficiaries paid in the current tax year to date of death and the previous tax year.

It is also helpful to contact the Recovery from Estates division of the Department of Work and Pensions where the deceased was in receipt of means tested benefits to ensure that there are no refunds due to the Department of Work and Pensions for incorrectly claimed benefits. The cross over to incorrectly claimed benefits can occur whereby the deceased entered long term nursing care and cancellation of benefits such as attendance allowance were not undertaken prior to the deceased's death.

Private Pensions

Depending on the nature of the pension scheme, it is likely that other than a week or two's pension falling due to the estate, the remainder of the pension will fall outwith the estate.

The payment of death benefits from most private pensions now fall outwith the estate and will be at the discretion of the pension trustees. Not all schemes will fall out with the estate though and therefore you should check with the scheme provider before making that assumption. Where the pension falls out with the estate, this does not mean that you do not have to deal with the pension. In most cases, you will still need to supply the death certificate, a copy of the Will and details of the close relatives of the deceased. You will also need to advise whether there was anyone financially dependent on the deceased such as a spouse or civil partner or minor children to enable the pension provider to make a decision regarding who is entitled to what from the death benefits of the pension.

While many people put in a place a nomination form or expression of wishes form to determine who should inherit the death benefits from the pension, this is by no means guaranteed and the pension trustees have the ability to settle the pension benefits with whomever they see fit.

Please note that discretionary benefit awards on death by the pension trustees need to be dealt with within 2 years of death otherwise a hefty tax charge will be applied. Therefore while the pension and its death benefit may not form part of the estate, it is best to ensure that any information requested by the pension provider is given to the provider as soon as possible to enable them to make their decision and settle the benefit with the recipient(s).

Membership Cards

Membership cards will let you identify groups that the deceased may have joined. Any paid for memberships will need to be cancelled and you may find that a partial refund will be due to the estate.

Loyalty schemes

It is always worth writing away to loyalty schemes as sometimes accrued points and vouchers can be transferred to a beneficiary.

Trusts

Where the deceased was a beneficiary of a trust, you will need to identify the type of trust and the nature of the deceased's entitlement from the trust as depending on the entitlement (which could be capital, income or both), this may mean that the value of the trust will need to be aggregated with the value of the estate at date of death and Inheritance Tax assessed against the total value of the combined estate and trust. This could result in the estate paying Inheritance Tax where it would not otherwise be payable due to the size of the estate.

Other Estates

Where the deceased was entitled to a legacy or share of another estate, you will need to establish what is left to be transferred to the deceased, for example, income generated to the date of their death or capital balance as this will form part of the deceased's estate.

Credit cards

Before you write to a credit card company to advise of the death, make sure you check with the family to see whether there are any extra cards on the credit account. This is because the credit card company will cancel all cards on the account on notification of the death where it is the principal card holder that has died which may leave a spouse or child or other dependant without access to funds if they were a card holder on the account. This can be a particular problem where there is no joint bank account or where a joint bank account has insufficient funds to support the card holder and the sole accounts are frozen pending receipt of Probate.

On notification of death, the credit card company will normally freeze the account so that no further interest accrues. If there is a debit balance which is due to be paid by the estate and the credit card company is also the deceased's bank, they will usually settle the balance from the funds held in the deceased's bank account before it is closed or in part if the debt exceeds the balance held in the bank accounts.

Loans and Mortgages

These can usually be identified from the direct debits or standing orders details supplied by the deceased's bank. The lender will be able to confirm the sums due at the date of death and depending on the lender, they may freeze the interest accruing for a period of time to give the Personal Representatives time to administer the estate.

As with credit cards, where the lender is also the deceased's bank, the balance may be cleared from the deceased's bank accounts before any excess balance is paid over to the estate.

Historically some mortgage providers enabled the mortgage account to remain open with a nominal balance showing as due in order that they could retain the title deeds safely on behalf of the client. There may not therefore be a direct debit on the deceased's account for you to identify the security holder. You can check if a mortgage is held by checking the title deeds on the Land Register. In any event, you will need this information to discharge the security prior to the property being sold or transferred to a beneficiary.

Mail order

You will need to check whether the deceased had any mail order accounts for example with Next, Very, Littlewoods etc. If there are no direct debits or standing orders showing and nothing which has come through by a mail redirection, another way to check whether the deceased had such an account is to look back over the deceased's bank statements to see if there are any card payments to such vendors.

Utilities

You will usually be able to locate the deceased's utility providers through the direct debits section of their bank account. If no direct debits can be located, you can trace their gas and electric suppliers online[42].

Council Tax

Where the deceased was the sole occupier of the property, an exemption can usually be obtained for 6 months to give the Personal Representatives time to administer the estate. Where the property hasn't been capable of being sold during that time, it will ultimately depend on the council as to whether they will continue to apply a full exemption or apply a reduced rate of council tax. Where the property is lying empty for a long time, penalty council tax may apply.

---

[42] https://www.ofgem.gov.uk/information-consumers/energy-advice-households/finding-your-energy-supplier-or-network-operator

Where after the death, there is a single adult continuing to reside at the property, a single person's exemption should be applied for to reduce that person's council tax.

Mail Redirection

You should consider whether a mail redirection should be put on the deceased's property where it is lying empty. While many asset holders and lenders are putting accounts online, particularly where your deceased has been an elderly person, they may still receive paper statements which will help you track down assets.

Lost bank account search

This is a free useful tool from the British Bankers Association which enables you to check for dormant bank accounts. You complete the details online and the banks, building societies and National Savings and Investments will check their records and come back to you. While in my experience 9 times out of 10 there will be nothing to be found, my biggest hit on using this service led to me finding around £450,000 with Santander when there had been no paperwork in the house whatsoever which indicated an account with them. Likewise for another estate, I found around £250,000 in dormant accounts as a consequence of using this service. More often than not, the results that will come back will be for Premium Bonds which will quite frequently have been bought several decades ago when it was common to buy Premium Bonds as a gift on the birth of a child or for a 21st birthday.

Intellectual Property

Intellectual property can include trademarks, copyright and patents and is a separate right distinct from the work it relates to e.g. an author publishes a book for people to read but retains the copyright to the work so that it cannot be reproduced without permission.

As Intellectual property may subsist for many years after the date of the death, this can cause issues as depending on the age of the appointed Personal Representative, they may not survive the requisite period to fulfil the administration of the estate!

You will also need to check that in relation to registered design rights and trademarks that deadlines for renewing do not get missed during the administration of the estate.

Digital Assets

Digital Assets are things such as bitcoin, social media accounts, domain addresses and email accounts. If the deceased did not leave a paper trail of their digital assets, it can be near impossible to identify digital assets in the estate. Particularly in the case of bitcoin, where details of how to access the asset have not been left, it can mean that the asset becomes inaccessible which can mean a significant loss of value to the estate.

Crofts

One would not expect you to come across a croft in a run of the mile estate in your career but it can happen. Crofts are parcels of land which are specific to Scotland and have danger written all over them! Where there is a croft involved in your estate, you will need to ascertain what type of croft you are dealing with as this will determine how you proceed with dealing with the croft later in the administration. In any event you will need to have the croft or the tenancy thereof valued at the date of death. You should at the outset consider enlisting a specialist Scottish Solicitor to assist with the crofting aspects as there are many traps for the unwary when dealing with crofts which can result in the entitlement to the croft being lost or indeed the croft landing with the wrong person due to the incorrect drafting of the Will.

The types of crofts are as follows:

Owner occupied croft – this is a type of croft whereby the person is the owner of a croft, was the crofter of the land at the time it was acquired or acquired title as the nominee of the crofter or otherwise through succession laws or purchased the croft from the landlord and a new croft was created and that the croft has not been let out as a croft by the owner.

Croft tenancy – the asset here is the tenancy rather than the land and buildings itself which can in some instances be highly valuable. The tenancy may be of land or land plus buildings. The deceased will either be the tenant or the landlord (although the Landlord is more often than not likely to be either the Scottish government or an Estate).

Decrofted land – land and/or buildings which were previously subject to crofting law but have been taken out of the crofting law remit by a voluntary process. This land is treated like any other land and/or property with no special procedures required.

In addition to narrating the extent of the tenancy and/or the land and buildings, you will also need to identify whether there are any livestock included (referred to as a souming) which needs to be attended too. This can be identified from either the Crofting Register[43] or the Register of Crofts[44] depending on where the croft is registered.

Where there is a testate estate, you have 12 months from the date of death to transfer the croft tenancy to the beneficiary. Where there is an intestate estate, this timeframe is extended to 24 months. If the deadline is missed, you will need to obtain agreement from the Landlord to extend the timeframe. Please note that an extension to the time frame is not automatic and therefore estates involving crofts should be expedited as much as possible to avoid falling foul of the timescales. If the transfer takes too long, the tenancy can be marketed by the Crofting Commission. It is however possible to have such marketing put on hold where you can prove that the administration of the estate is moving although it is by no means guaranteed that the Commission will agree to it.

A point to note is that if there is a crofting tenancy in a testate estate it can only be bequeathed to a single individual or two or more individuals where each has a right to the whole tenancy and no part of the croft would become untenanted as a result of the bequest. Where this gets tricky is where a testator tries to split a croft in a Will e.g. field A to son and house to daughter. As crofted tenancy law is a particularly difficult area of law to navigate, it is worth getting an independent opinion from a crofting specialist to make sure that any bequests are valid and to

---

[43] https://www.crofts.ros.gov.uk/register/search

[44] https://www.crofting.scotland.gov.uk/register-of-crofts

confirm who is entitled to it in the event that the bequest in the Will is found to be invalid. This is not the case with owner occupied crofts which can be bequeathed to any number of people who would all become joint owners.

Where there are livestock involved, you will need to obtain a valuation for them as well as any farming equipment which is not otherwise contained in the valuation of the crofting business.

A practical pointer for crofts involving livestock (and indeed for farms) is to make sure they are being looked after or otherwise sold off at the earliest possible opportunity. The last thing you need to be dealing with during the administration of the estate is the disposal of dead animals!

<u>General</u>

In all cases, you should always ask assets holders as part of initial investigations if there are any other products held with them, either in the sole name of the deceased or jointly with another to ensure that you have caught all assets.

CHAPTER EIGHT

ASSETS WRITTEN
IN TRUST

Trust assets are normally separate entities distinct from estates. There are however certain circumstances whereby you will need to deal with trust assets as part of the estate administration process.

<u>Assets written in Trust</u>

Frequently, life policies and bonds are written in trust on the advice of financial advisers. The trusts used to hold the assets are frequently 'off the shelf trusts' which have been provided by the asset provider as opposed to a bespoke trust which has been drafted by a solicitor. These products will usually have had their assets written in trust and promptly forgotten about until the death occurs. You will usually find out about the trust when you write to the life insurance company and they advise that they cannot provide you with any information relating to the policy as it is written in trust.

When this happens, you need to contact the asset holder and ask for the details of the trustees as you will need certain information from the trustees in order to properly report the estate to HMRC. The asset holder will normally either provide you with the contact details or they will allow you to send a letter addressed to the trustees to them for them to pass on.

Information you need to know about a trust which was settled by the deceased to administer your estate is as follows:

- Who the current trustees are

- A copy of the trust deed

- Date of settlement

- The dates and amounts of settlements into the trust by the deceased as these will need to be assessed for gift reporting for Inheritance Tax purposes.

Where the deceased was the beneficiary of a trust, you will need to ascertain the following:

- The type of trust, with particular reference to whether the value of the trust requires to be aggregated with the value of the deceased's estate for the purposes of assessing Inheritance Tax;

- Whether there are any sums due to the deceased from the trust that had not been paid over in full prior to the death

Where the trust deed refers to instructions that can be provided by the deceased as either settlor or beneficiary by Will, you will also need to share a copy of the Will with the trustees so that they can manage the trust effectively.

Last trustee standing

Where you are advised or discover that the deceased is the last trustee of a trust, nothing can happen with the trust assets until Probate to the estate is obtained. Once Probate to the estate has been obtained, the deceased's Personal Representatives will then acquire a power of appointment to appoint trustees[45] to be able to handle the trust estate, notwithstanding that the trust assets do not form part of the estate nor will not necessarily be distributed according to the terms of the deceased's Will.

When trusts can trigger Inheritance Tax in an estate

There are situations in which the death of a beneficiary of a trust can trigger a charge to Inheritance Tax in an estate. This will occur where the deceased was a beneficiary of one of the following types of trusts:

---

[45] S36(1) and S36(4) Trustee Act 1925

1. A bare trust is a trust in which the assets are controlled by the trustees but which ultimately belong to one or more beneficiaries. It is a structure that is frequently used for minor beneficiaries in which the trustees control the assets until the child becomes 18 and thereafter the beneficiary can direct what happens to the trust fund.

2. An immediate post death life interest trust is one which is created on death under the terms of a Will. It grants the life tenant (who will be our deceased for these purposes) the right to enjoy the income of the trust fund but they will never (usually) own the capital of the trust.

3. A trust for a vulnerable beneficiary is a trust with a valid vulnerable beneficiary election[46]. It can apply to trusts set up for children under 18 by their parent who has died or trusts set up for disabled persons eligible for certain state benefits[47] (although interestingly, they do not need to be in actual receipt of the same – just meet the eligibility criteria which begs the question that if the person was eligible surely they ought to be making a claim but that is something to ponder another time!).

4. A personal injury trust is a trust that is set up to hold the award compensation from a personal injury settlement. The purpose of the trust is to put the funds outwith the recipient's estate for the purposes of being assessed for means tested benefits. The settlor is the person who has been injured and must be able to obtain a benefit from the trust. As the funds in the trust had been paid out to compensate the recipient for certain losses be it limbs, ability to work etc, the trust is usually (but please check the trust deed for its terms as it is not automatic) not subject to the usual

---

[46] https://www.gov.uk/government/publications/trusts-and-estates-vulnerable-person-election-form-vpe1

[47] At the time of drafting of this book, attendance allowance, disability living allowance, personal independent payment, increased disablement pension, constant attendance allowance, armed forces independence payment and child disability payment

discretionary trust tax regime and has the (usually) more favourable personal tax treatment that applies to the settlor/beneficiary. Please note that a personal injury trust may also qualify as a trust for vulnerable beneficiary.

In all of the above situations, the value of the trust at the time of the death will be aggregated with the value of the beneficiary's estate. Where the combination of the personal estate and trust assets exceed the nil rate band, Inheritance Tax at the estate rate of 40% will be payable on the excess (less any applicable allowances and reliefs). The Inheritance Tax due is thereafter paid pro rata between the trust and the estate and settled from the respective trust and estate assets before distribution to the respective beneficiaries takes place.

Gifts

Settlements into trust may require to be called back into account when calculating the Inheritance Tax due on estate.

Where a chargeable lifetime transfer has been made into a trust which exceeds the nil rate band and the Settlor dies within 7 years of making the settlement, Inheritance Tax will fall due on the balance above the nil rate band. In these circumstances, the Settlor will normally have paid Inheritance Tax at the time of settlement at a rate of 20% on the balance above the nil rate band. This 20% lifetime tax charge will act as a credit towards the applicable estate rate of Inheritance Tax which falls due on the balance of the settlement. The 7 year rule can extend to 14 years via the operation of the backwards Shadow (see Inheritance Tax chapter for further information).

CHAPTER NINE

TYPES OF GRANT

As much as we have all come across the situation whereby the beneficiary cannot understand why they have not received their share of the estate when Granny died yesterday, it is not possible for a Grant of Probate to be issued within seven days of the date of death. Where a Grant of Administration is required, this time frame extends to 14 days48.

As previously mentioned, depending on the value of each asset in the estate and the various encashment limits that each asset holder applies to the amount of asset held with them that they will release without sight of a Grant, it may well be possible to ingather an estate without the need to apply for a Grant. However, should a Grant be required because there is a property which does not automatically pass to the survivor or where the value of an asset is held with an asset holder that requires a Grant before release, you will need to ascertain what type of Grant is required.

Regular Grants

There are 3 types of regular Grants:

1. Probate

2. Letters of Administration with Will annexed

3. Letters of Administration

---

[48] R6 (2) Non-Contentious Probate Rules 1987

Who can take out a Grant?

Probate

This is a Testate Grant. A Grant of Probate can only be applied for by the named Executors in a Will and/or Codicil. This can be an express appointment in a particular format or an indirect appointment where the usual Executor's appointment clause isn't used but words indicating that the person should take up the position are used for example "I want X to distribute my estate". A Grant cannot be taken in the name of the Executor in the following circumstances:

- where the Executor survives the deceased but dies before the Grant is obtained;

- the Executor fails to appear to a citation; or

- the Executor has renounced Probate

Letters of Administration with Will Annexed

This is a Testate Grant where there is no Executor who is capable and willing to obtain Probate, for example, where the Executors have all predeceased the deceased, then Letters of Administration with Will annexed must be sought. This procedure can be used in the following circumstances:

- The express or implied Executors named in the Will have predeceased the deceased;

- The express or implied Executors named in the Will have renounced their entitlement to obtain Probate;

- The express or implied Executors named in the Will survived the deceased but have died before the Grant can be obtained;

- No Executor has not been expressly or impliedly appointed in the Will;

- The Executor(s) expressly or impliedly named in the Will fails to appear to a citation; or

- The Executor(s) expressly or impliedly named in the Will is a minor. In this case the minor cannot obtain a Grant until he/she is 18 years old. Where in these circumstances, if the Administration of the estate cannot wait until the Executor turns 18, then a parental or guardian application may be made on the minor's behalf. Once they reach the age of 18 years old, a Cessate Grant can be applied for by the former minor to deal with the remainder of the Administration of the estate. If there are more Executors than the minor appointed and at least one of them is an adult, then an application by the adult Executor will be preferred to a parental or guardian application on behalf of the minor49.

Letters of Administration

This is the Grant used to administer intestate estates.

Clearing off of Executors

For Letters of Administration, there is a process of clearing off of Executors which must take place to ascertain who is entitled to take the Grant. The order of preference is set out in R22 Non-Contentious Probate Rules 1987 as follows:

1. the surviving husband, wife or civil partner of the deceased;

2. the children of the deceased and the issue of any deceased child who died before the deceased;

3. the parents of the deceased;

---

49 R27 (5) Non-Contentious Probate Rules 1987

4.   brothers and sisters of the whole blood and the issue of any deceased brother or sister of the whole blood who died before the deceased;

5.   brothers and sisters of the half blood and the issue of any deceased brother or sister of the half-blood who died before the deceased;

6.   grandparents;

7.   uncles and aunts of the whole blood and the issue of any deceased uncle or aunt of the whole blood who died before the deceased;

8.   uncles and aunts of the half blood and the issue of any deceased uncle or aunt of the half-blood who died before the deceased.

9.   If all persons entitled to a Grant under the foregoing provisions of this rule have been cleared off, a Grant may be made to a creditor of the deceased or to any person who, notwithstanding that they have no immediate beneficial interest in the estate, may have a beneficial interest in the event of an accretion thereto.

10. In default of any of the foregoing persons having a beneficial interest in the estate, the Treasury Solicitor shall be entitled to a Grant bona vacantia on behalf of the Crown.

All persons in the same class have an equal right to take out the Grant but everyone in the same class must be removed before anyone from the next class down can take the Grant. The Personal Representative of a person in any of the classes above shall have the same right to a Grant as the person to whom he represents[50].

---

[50] An alive member of a lower class than the surviving spouse/civil partner shall be preferred to the personal representative of a spouse who has died without taking a beneficial interest in the whole estate of the deceased as ascertained at the time of the application for the grant.

For Letters of Administration with Will annexed, one of more beneficiaries will take out the Grant to administer the estate in accordance with the Will. There is a set order of precedence about who can take out the Grant as follows[51]:

1. any residuary legatee or devisee holding in trust for any other person;

2. any other residuary legatee or devisee (including one for life) or where the residue is not wholly disposed of by the will, any person entitled to share in the undisposed of residue (including the Treasury Solicitor when claiming bona vacantia on behalf of the Crown), provided that—

    a. unless a registrar otherwise directs, a residuary legatee or devisee whose legacy or devise is vested in interest shall be preferred to one entitled on the happening of a contingency, and

    b. where the residue is not in terms wholly disposed of, the registrar may, if he is satisfied that the testator has nevertheless disposed of the whole or substantially the whole of the known estate, allow a Grant to be made to any legatee or devisee entitled to, or to share in, the estate so disposed of, without regard to the persons entitled to share in any residue not disposed of by the will;

3. the Personal Representative of any residuary legatee or devisee (but not one for life, or one holding in trust for any other person), or of any person entitled to share in any residue not disposed of by the will;

4. any other legatee or devisee (including one for life or one holding in trust for any other person) or any creditor of the deceased, provided that, unless a registrar otherwise directs, a legatee or

---

[51] R20 Non-Contentious Probate Rules 1987

devisee whose legacy or devise is vested in interest shall be preferred to one entitled on the happening of a contingency;

5. the Personal Representative of any other legatee or devisee (but not one for life or one holding in trust for any other person) or of any creditor of the deceased.

Chain Of Representation of Executors

This is a mechanism used to ensure that administration of estates do not come to a grinding halt in the event of the death of the Executor. This is utilised in circumstances where a sole accepting Executor or sole surviving Executor of a deceased dies having obtained a Grant but also leaving a Will of their own, then the Executor's Executor will then also become the Executor of the original deceased's estate and so on. In these circumstances no further Grant is required to the original deceased's estate and title is shown to the original deceased's estate by production of the original Grant and all subsequent Grants thereafter of deceased Executors and their deceased Executors and so on. The ability to administer the original deceased's estate comes from the chain of Grant. The chain of representation however only applies to testate estates.

In intestate estates there no such chain of representation notwithstanding that the now deceased Executor of the original deceased died testate. It will be necessary for the new administrator to apply to the court for Letters of Administration De Bonis Non Administratis to deal with the un-administered assets.

The chain of representation of Executors ceases as soon as one of the Executors dies intestate.

Special Grants

Sometimes, a regular Grant will not be appropriate in the estate you are administering. In these circumstances, a special Grant will be required.

De Bonis Non Administratis

To use this Grant, the person who originally received the Grant must have died leaving assets in the original estate unadministered. It applies to both estates with Grants of Probate and Letters of Administration (with Will Annexed). Where Probate has been Granted, this type of Grant can only be used where the chain of representation of Executors has been broken (namely, the last Personal Representative in place died intestate).

Ad Colligenda Bona

This is a very specific and limited Grant for ingathering specific assets. This is used in circumstances where an application for a full Grant cannot be made for example where it is unclear who should be appointed as a Personal Representative or where the full extent of the estate cannot yet be ascertained e.g. where an investigation is required to repatriate stolen assets into an estate. This is a particularly useful Grant where there may be a property that needs to be sold or stocks and shares that need to be sold quickly in a falling market. In any event, the Grant will cease immediately once an application for a full Grant is made be that an application by the person in whose favour the current Grant is made or another person.

Pendente Lite

This type of Grant is used where there is a dispute regarding the terms of the estate. This type of Grant is normally issued to a person who has been mutually agreed upon by the parties at dispute or has court proceedings already in play or a person nominated by the Court. Where there is no pressing need to administer an estate, this Grant should not be used. It however can be used in the circumstances where a situation has arisen that an estate requires to be protected or is otherwise at risk of loss if no one can administer the estate e.g. an investment portfolio falling in value in a falling market. Unlike a full Grant, this type of Grant gives the holder no power to distribute. It simply lets them undertake the specific act upon which the Grant was founded.

Application for such a Grant is made by summons to the Master of the Chancery Division and thereafter if satisfied, the application should be made to the Principal Registry.

Durante Absentia

This is another type of limited Grant which enables a creditor or any other person with an interest to make progress with the estate where the one-year anniversary of the deceased's death has passed and the person(s) to whom a Grant has been made is/are currently resident out with England and Wales.

Durante Minore Aetate

This Grant is used where the sole Executor is a minor[52]. The Grant can be taken by the following:

1. An adult residuary beneficiary; or

2. Where the minor is also a residuary beneficiary, the Grant is taken by two people, at least one of whom must be the parent or legal guardian.

The Grant ceases on the minor becoming an adult and the former minor will need to obtain Double Probate to continue the estate.

Double Probate

This is where a Grant has already been issued and occurs where power has been reserved to an Executor. This enables the Executor who had power reserved to then obtain a Grant in his/her own name at a later stage.

---

[52] S118 Supreme Court Act 1981

Reservation of power occurs when an Executor does not want or is not able to take out Probate but also does not want to resign their position. Circumstances were power may be reserved:

1. an Executor who had been a minor is not capable of taking out a Grant, and therefore if the minor was appointed along with an adult as Executor, the adult could have Probate Granted in their sole favour with power reserved to the minor. If any part of the estate remains unadministered by the time the minor Executor reaches 18 years old, the now adult Executor can in turn apply for the Grant of Double Probate to be brought on as an Executor with title;

2. there may be more than four Executors appointed in which case only four can go forward to be named in the Grant. Note however that in this specific case, in order for another Executor outwith the original 4 to seek a Grant, one or more of the original Executors must have died or resigned or otherwise be unable to act as there can only ever be a maximum of four Executors on a Grant at any one time; or

3. an Executor may not, for example, feel up to dealing with paperwork following the death and may be happy for a co-Executor to take a Grant without them.

Reservation of power is a useful tool and provides a 'back up' in case something happens to any one or more of the Executors who have sought the original Grant.

Cessate Grant

This type of Grant applies where the original Grant was limited in time (for example, where a Grant Durante Minore Aetate has been taken out) and that time limit has expired. This can occur in the following circumstances:

•   Where a Grant has been taken out on behalf of a minor Executor;

- Where an Executor has been appointed for life and dies prior to the estate being administered in full in which case any other Executor can apply for the Grant or failing which, any other person in the order of clearing off of Executors;

- Where a previously mentally incapable adult recovers from their illness and can administer the remainder of the estate; or

- Where the Grant was originally taken out by an Attorney, and the Granter of the Power of Attorney wishes to take the Attorney's place to administer the remainder of the estate.

CHAPTER TEN

SETTLED LAND

With any luck, you will only come across this situation once in a blue moon as it has not been possible to create a new settled land provision since 31 December 1996[53].

A settlement for these purposes is one that complies with the Settled Land Act 1925. The legislation was designed to keep a property within a certain family line upon life interest.

A settled land provision creates a strict settlement in which a person has a life interest in the land, usually in the title deeds to the property but it could also be created by a Will. Unlike usual life interests whereby the legal title to the trust assets is vested in the trustees, in a settled land provision, the legal title is vested in the life tenant. Title deeds should always be checked to ascertain if this provision applies to the land in hand. This should not be confused with a trust for sale which already vests in the Trustees[54]. Where you have a Settled Land provision, there will essentially be two Grants of Probate needed – one to deal with the non-settled land assets and one to deal with the settled land assets.

The Settled Land Grant is restricted to the extent of the settled land. The effect of the Grant is to provide that the title to the land can move on. The Grant is limited to the extent of the settled land. In this case, the PRs are known as Special Personal Representatives.

The deceased's estate Grant is restricted to all assets save for the settled land.

---

[53] Trusts of Land and Appointment of Trustees Act 1996 (also referred to as TOLATA)

[54] And which now occurs from 1 January 1997 through TOLATA

The order and type of Grants needed depends on who does what and when.

- Where the trustees of the Settled Land take out a Settled Land Grant before the Personal Representatives of the deceased take out a Grant to the deceased's estate, then the Personal Representatives of the deceased will take out a "Caeterorium" Grant.

- Where the trustees of the Settled Land take out a Settled Land Grant after the Personal Representatives of the deceased take out a Grant to the deceased's estate, then the Personal Representatives of the deceased will take out a "Save and Except" Grant

Both the "Caeterorium" Grant and "Save and Except" Grant do the same thing – effectively excluding the land contained with the Settled Land Grant. The procedure to obtain Probate or Letters of Administration will be taken as normal following the usual testate or intestate procedures as appropriate. The type of Grant simply reflects the timing of when the Personal Representatives of the deceased's estate took out the Grant. You can detail the type of application needed at 2.12, 2.15 & 2.16 of the Probate Application for professionals[55].

Where your deceased is the last life tenant and on his/her death, the property vests in the remainderman (the ultimate beneficiary of the trust), then a Settled Land Grant is not required and the ability to take the Grant will vest in the in the Personal Representatives of the deceased's estate.

---

https://assets.publishing.service.gov.uk/government/uploads/system/upload s/attachment_data/file/1075221/PA1P_0422_practitioner_save.pdf

CHAPTER ELEVEN

APPLYING FOR
THE GRANT

Once you have identified the extent of the estate, the debts of the deceased and the type of Grant needed, you can apply for the Grant.

Timescales to obtain a Grant

Current turnaround times per the Probate Registry are stated as being around 16 weeks to process a Grant application[56]. If you have Inheritance Tax to pay, you can add another 4-5 weeks into the beginning of that timeframe for HMRC to process the IHT400 and send over the IHT421 to the Probate Registry. All in, it is not currently a quick process[57] and something which you should make your clients aware of as this can have a knock-on effect on the ability to sell investments and property and generally impact their ability to ingather and distribute the estate.

STEP ONE – Is the estate subject to Inheritance Tax?

You will need to identify whether the estate is subject to Inheritance Tax before you begin the Grant application as you will need to follow different processes depending on the outcome.

---

[56] At December 2022

[57] Although one would hope we shall soon be out of the Covid19 backlog

A) **There is Inheritance Tax to pay**

Applying for an Inheritance Tax reference

If the estate is subject to Inheritance Tax, you will need to apply for an Inheritance Tax reference at least 3 weeks prior to needing to pay the Inheritance Tax on the estate and apply for the Grant. This can be done online[58] or by post[59] using form IHT422. If you can do so, use the online system to obtain the reference number if for no other reason than you will know that your application has actually made it into the system as you will receive a confirmation email. *Do not apply for an Inheritance Tax reference if your estate is exempt from Inheritance Tax.*

Paying Inheritance Tax

The Inheritance Tax due on the estate will need to be paid prior to applying for the Grant. This leads to a bit of a chicken and egg situation as the Inheritance Tax needs to be paid before applying for the Grant but the personal representative cant get access to the assets until after the Grant. Your Personal Representatives may be lucky and have access to sufficient funds to pay the Inheritance Tax due, for example, where banks have a higher threshold to close accounts than £5,000 and have released funds without sight of a Grant. In other situations where the balance is too high to be released without a Grant, the asset holder may take part in the direct payments scheme. This is a scheme whereby on receipt of a completed form IHT423[60], the asset holder will release funds from the assets directly to HMRC in settlement of the Inheritance Tax due. You can apply to multiple assets holders to release funds under this scheme.

Form IHT400 and supplementary pages (which is the Inheritance Tax return) must be received by HMRC by the one-year anniversary otherwise penalties will accrue. You can however write to HMRC with

---

[58] https://www.tax.service.gov.uk/shortforms/form/CAR_IHT_Pre_Ref

[59] https://www.gov.uk/government/publications/inheritance-tax-application-for-an-inheritance-tax-reference-iht422

[60] https://www.gov.uk/government/publications/inheritance-tax-direct-payment-scheme-bank-or-building-society-account-iht423

mitigating circumstances (for example, an Executor that wouldn't progress the estate or estate assets that required to be traced across multiple jurisdictions) and they may waive the penalties.

You can pay Inheritance Tax interest free up till 6 months have elapsed from the date of death. Thereafter interest will accrue until payment is made in full[61].

HMRC appreciates that not all assets are readily realisable and therefore while all Inheritance Tax needs to be paid on moveable assets such as bank accounts, investments and personal effects, only 10% of the Inheritance Tax due on land and buildings needs to be paid before the Grant can be obtained. Thereafter the balance can either be paid in annual instalments of 10% or it is paid in full once the land/buildings have been transferred or sold following receipt of the Grant. Where the instalment option is selected, if all of the Inheritance Tax due has not been paid within the first 6 months, interest will run on the balance until it is paid in full.

If the estate is land rich but moveable asset poor and there are insufficient funds available within the estate or via the direct payment scheme, it may be necessary for the Executors to take out a loan to meet the balance of Inheritance Tax due. This can be done in one of 3 ways:

1. Where a beneficiary has sufficient funds to do so, they may lend the estate money to cover the Inheritance Tax due on whatever terms they see fit;

2. Where an Executor/Administrator has sufficient funds to do so, they may lend the estate money to cover the Inheritance Tax due on whatever terms they see fit; or

---

[61] HMRC have a handy worksheet to help you work out the interest due – see https://assets.publishing.service.gov.uk/government/uploads/system/uploads/attachment_data/file/734666/IHT400_Helpsheet.pdf or search "Working out the interest on Inheritance Tax payments" in your browser

3. The Executor may need to seek a loan on commercial terms from a traditional lender such as a bank.

If it proves to be impossible to obtain a loan at all (and not just non acceptance of an offer because of poor commercial terms), then you will need to send evidence of the Executor's endeavours to secure a loan (including all notifications of knock backs) to HMRC to see if they will agree to process the Grant without Inheritance Tax being paid up front. There would need to be incredibly exceptional circumstances for a loan of some description not to be available to the Executors.

Declaring Inheritance Tax

You will need to prepare the Inheritance Tax return using form IHT400 and supplemental forms. The IHT400 is the summary of the asset of the asset and the Tax position. The supplemental forms provide additional information for HMRC on the nature of the asset and any reliefs being claimed. The available supplemental forms are as follows:

1. IHT401 – Domicile outside the UK

2. IHT402 – Transferable nil rate band claim form

3. IHT403 – Gifts and other transfers of value

4. IHT404 – Jointly owned assets

5. IHT405 – Houses, land and buildings

6. IHT406 – Bank and building society accounts

7. IHT407 – Household and personal effects

8. IHT408 – Household and personal effects donated to charity

9. IHT409 – Pensions

10. IHT410 – Life assurance and annuities

11. IHT411 – Listed stocks and shares

12. IHT412 – Unlisted stocks and shares

13. IHT413 – Business and partnership assets

14. IHT414 – Agricultural relief

15. IHT415 – Interest in another estate

16. IHT416 – Debts due to the estate

17. IHT417 – Foreign assets

18. IHT418 – Assets held in trust

19. IHT419 – Debts owned by the deceased

20. IHT420 – National heritage, conditional exemption and maintenance

21. IHT421 – Probate summary

22. IHT422 – Application for an Inheritance Tax reference number

23. IHT423 – Direct payment scheme form

24. IHT430 – Reduced rate of Inheritance Tax claim form

25. IHT435 – Residence nil rate band claim form

26. IHT436 – Transferable residence nil rate band claim form

The supplemental forms that need to be completed will be different for every estate and will be dictated by the nature of the assets that are contained within your estate and the reliefs being claimed. Leave yourself a good couple of hours of peace and quiet to complete the IHT400 and supplementary forms so that you do not miss anything or double count an asset. There is an excellent manual that has been prepared by HMRC to assist with completing the forms[62].

TIP – if you are tasked with the preparation or revision of initial investigation template letters for your firm, it would be worthwhile taking some time to go through each of the IHT400 and supplemental forms to find out what information may be needed from each type of asset holder to be able to complete the forms. Thereafter, you can incorporate requests into your template letters for the information needed thus streamlining the information gathering exercise.

---

[62] For deaths on or after 1 January 2022 use https://assets.publishing.service. gov.uk/government/uploads/system/uploads/attachment_data/file/111815 4/IHT400-Notes-English-2022.pdf. For deaths on or before 31 December 2021, use https://assets.publishing.service.gov.uk/government/uploads/ system/uploads/attachment_data/file/1046019/IHT4002021-Notes-11- 21-online.pdf. Be careful to select the correct manual as there are differences depending on when the person died.

TIP – when completing an IHT400, I prepare an inventory of the assets within the estate on Excel. I then rearrange the assets into the order that they need to be listed on the IHT400. This enables me to split assets where necessary (for example, where there is a portfolio of shares with dividends due but not paid at the date of death, the shares will go in box 63 of the IHT400 and the dividends will go in Box 64 of the IHT400) and also ensure that I have accounted for all assets and they are in the right place e.g.

Box No	Description	Total	Box Total
51	51 Acacia Avenue, Banana Land	£250,000	£250,000
52	Virgin Money Account no: 00000/12345678 Balance	£100,000	
	Royal Bank of Scotland Account no: 00000/87654321 Balance	£100,000	£200,000

You can also use papers apart to the supplemental forms to provide the information requested, for example, where you have too many of the asset to fit into the boxes. You can also provide formal valuations such as Probate stocks and shares valuations as part of the supplemental information.

TIP – The IHT400 will round the numbers input. Cross check your inventory against the final numbers in the form to make sure nothing has been omitted. They should come to within a £1 or two of each other on rounding.

The IHT400 and supplementary forms along with Form IHT421[63] should be completed prior to completing the Grant application. Both the Inheritance Tax forms and Grant application should be signed at the same time.

The IHT400, supplementary forms and IHT421 are thereafter sent to HMRC on or after the Inheritance Tax has been paid or the funds have been requested using the direct payments scheme. Once HMRC receives the funds, they will forward the stamped IHT421 to the Probate Registry in order that the Grant application can proceed. Where an IHT400 has been submitted to HMRC, you should wait 20 working days after lodging it before submitting the Grant application[64].

B) **There is no Inheritance Tax to pay**

Where the deceased died before 31 December 2021, and there is no Inheritance Tax to pay, you will also need to complete and submit with the Grant application either:

1. Form IHT207[65]; or

2. Form IHT205[66].

Form IHT207 is used in circumstances where the deceased had their permanent home outside the UK and had less than £150,000 in cash and stocks and shares in the UK only. If they held any other type of asset and

---

[63] https://www.gov.uk/government/publications/inheritance-tax-inheritance-tax-account-iht400 To find the supplementary forms, search the form number in your browser e.g. "IHT403"

[64] https://www.gov.uk/government/publications/myhmcts-how-to-apply-for-probate-online/apply-for-probate-with-myhmcts#apply-with-letters-of-administration--with-an-annexed-will

[65] https://www.gov.uk/government/publications/inheritance-tax-return-of-estate-information-iht207-2006

[66] https://www.gov.uk/government/publications/inheritance-tax-return-of-estate-information-iht205-2011

in all other circumstances, you will need to use the IHT205. You may also need form IHT217[67] where a transferable nil rate band application is being made.

Where the deceased died on or after 1 January 2022 without Inheritance Tax being due, there are no additional forms to complete with the Grant application.

STEP TWO – Before you start a Grant application

Most Practitioner Grant applications must now be applied for online[68] using the My HMCTS portal. This is a different process to applying online through the lay person method. You can apply for an account at https://www.gov.uk/guidance/myhmcts-online-case-management-for-legal-professionals. An excellent manual to guide you through the process from creation of a case to submitting a case on the My HMCTS portal and then tracking its progress through to the Grant is available[69].

---

[67] https://www.gov.uk/government/publications/inheritance-tax-claim-to-transfer-unused-nil-rate-band-for-excepted-estates-iht217

[68] Since 2 November 2020 with the commencement of the Non-Contentious Probate (Amendment) Rules 2020. The exemptions which require a postal application are detailed at Schedule Three of the Rules.

[69] https://www.gov.uk/government/publications/myhmcts-how-to-apply-for-probate-online/apply-for-probate-with-myhmcts#before-you-start

STEP THREE – Applying for a Grant

Probate

Probate can be applied for online[70] or by post.

You will require form PA1P to apply for Probate[71].

There are two streams for applying for Probate:

1. Application by the Executor themselves; or

2. Practitioner route

It is not necessary for an Executor to instruct a Solicitor or Probate practitioner to apply for Probate but it would be beneficial to do so, if for no other reason than the correct type of Grant can be obtained and there should (famous last words!) be less chance of rejection at the Registry.

The form PA1P is a straight forward form that takes you through a series of questions to complete or skip as the case may be before reaching the declaration. The declaration on the form replaces the need for the former Oath for Probate.

When submitting the application (either by post or online), you will need to send the following original documents to HMCTS Probate, PO Box 12625, Harlow, CM20 9QE:

1. Death certificate. A Coroner's Interim Death certificate will also be accepted;

2. Will and any Codicils; and

---

[70] https://www.apply-for-probate.service.gov.uk/start-eligibility?_ga=2.218318046.676553771.1549454378-418831393.1545119317

[71] https://www.gov.uk/government/publications/form-pa1p-apply-for-probate-the-deceased-had-a-will

3. Where the deceased died on or prior to 31 December 2021 without inheritance Tax falling due, IHT205, IHT207 and/or IHT217.

Where Probate is applied for via postal application, you will also need to include the following:

1. the completed and signed PA1P form; and

2. a cheque made payable to "HM Courts and Tribunals Service" for the appropriate fees (remember to include the cost of any office copy certificates that you might need).

Letters of Administration

This process follows the process outlined above for Probate save that the application must be made online or by post using form PA1A[72].

Missing Will and/or Codicil

There are occasions upon which the original Will and/or Codicils go missing. This could be caused by something as simple as the family have put the document in the post to you and it has never arrived to the deceased signing the document at home and it going in lost in the post back to you. It could also be the case that a member of your staff has accidentally destroyed the original Will (guaranteed to give you at least one sleepless night when you discover that you cannot find a Will that you know was in your office!).

A missing testamentary writing may not preclude Probate from being obtained but It will certainly add a delay into obtaining the Grant. The procedure to be deployed in these circumstances depends on who is applying for the Grant:

1. Where the Executor themselves are applying for the Grant, they will need to complete and lodge Form PA13 which speaks to the

---

[72] https://www.gov.uk/government/publications/apply-for-probate-by-post-if-there-is-not-a-will

circumstances of the disappearance of the testamentary document.

2. Where a solicitor is acting, affidavit(s) will be required[73] speaking to the circumstances of the lost Will along with evidence, such as the recorded delivery number, copy of the Will from your file, who last had the Will etc.

The outcome will either be that a copy of the missing document will be admitted to the Probate or Letters with Administration with Will annexed process or further proof will require to be lead before a copy of the document can be led into the process.

<u>Fees</u>

Your firm will need to be registered with a HM Courts and Tribunals Service online fees account to be able to proceed with Grant applications[74].

Application fees for a Grant (including a limited Grant under the Settled Land rules) are currently[75] as follows:

1. Where the estate is less than £5,000, no fees are payable;

2. Where the estate exceeds £5,000, a £273 fee is payable;

3. Additional certificates can be obtained at £1.50 each and can be ordered at the same time of obtaining the Grant; and

4. Where double probate is being obtained, the application fee is £20 regardless of the size of the estate.

---

[73] R54 Non Contentious Probate Rules 1987

[74] Since 2 November 2020, most Practitioner cases need to be lodged online. The fee account can be obtained by registering the firm at https://www.gov.uk/government/publications/form-fee-account-application-form-fee-account-customer-application-form

[75] At December 2022

Assistance with fees is available for applicants that meet the following criteria:

1. Income element

    a. The applicant qualifies for one of the following state benefits:

        i. Income-based Jobseeker's Allowance (JSA)

        ii. Income-related Employment and Support Allowance (ESA)

        iii. Income Support

        iv. Universal Credit (and you earn less than £6,000 a year)

        v. Pension Credit (Guarantee Credit)

    b. The applicant is not in receipt of the above benefits but earns other income as follows:

        i. Up to £1,170 a month before tax for a single person;

        ii. Up to £1,345 a month before tax if the applicant has a partner[76].

2. Savings element

    a. The applicant is under 61 years old and has less than £3,000 in savings and investments; or

    b. The applicant can have up to £16,000 in savings and still qualify if:

---

[76] Both incomes thresholds for single and partnered applicants increase by £265 for each child the applicant has.

      i.   the fee they wish assistance with is between £1,000 and £10,000; or

     ii.   if the applicant or their partner are 61 and over.

The applicant must meet both the income and savings element criteria to qualify for financial assistance.

Applications for financial assistance can be lodged online or by post using form EX160[77].

---

[77] https://www.gov.uk/government/publications/apply-for-help-with-court-and-tribunal-fees

CHAPTER TWELVE

STOPPING A GRANT

There may be circumstances where you are not instructed by the Executors of the estate but by another party. Your client may have a competing interest to the purported Executor in the estate or may believe that there is a later Will or that the Will about to be entered into process has been unlawfully granted (for example through circumvention of the Testator's Will). Depending on the circumstances, you may wish to know when a Grant has been made or alternatively, stop the Grant being made.

Dispute

In cases where there is a dispute, for example, on the Will or who has title to take the Grant, a Caveat should be lodged. The Caveat will last 6 months and will enable the person lodging the Caveat to be notified when any application for a Grant is lodged with the Probate Registry. The application to lodge a Caveat can be done online[78] or by post using form PA8A[79].

The cost of lodging a Caveat is £3.00[80]

When the application for the Grant is made, the applicant will be advised of the Caveat. The Grant applicant can then issue a warning to the Caveat applicant which requires the Caveat applicant to make an appearance within 14 days. The effect of the warning is to move the administration of the estate forward – essentially the Caveat applicant must put up or

---

[78] https://www.gov.uk/stop-probate-application/apply-for-a-Caveat

[79] https://assets.publishing.service.gov.uk/government/uploads/system/uploads/attachment_data/file/1112982/PA8A_0922_save.pdf

[80] Correct as at November 2022

shut up. If the Probate Registrar agrees that the Caveat applicant has an interest that is contrary to that of the Grant applicant, the Caveat will remain in place and a hearing will be required to remove it.

If there is a vexatious Caveat lodged (bearing in mind that a person can lodge a Caveat without the assistance of a Solicitor and we all know how family relations can deteriorate rapidly after a death!), there is no contrary interest or the Caveat applicant fails to respond to the warning, then the Caveat can be removed.

A Caveat can also be extended if necessary, using Form PA8B[81].

Summons

In circumstances where there is no dispute as such as to the validity of the Will or clearing off of Executors, but for example, there may be concurrent interest, such as someone who is of equal ranking to the Grant applicant who wishes to be considered, the person may wish to have a summons issued. This cannot be lodged online and must be done through a paper application to the Leeds Probate Registry. The form to do so is not available online and must be obtained through Leeds Probate Registry[82]. The Registrar will then decide on who should be appointed to take forward the Grant.

---

[81] https://www.gov.uk/government/publications/apply-to-extend-a-caveat-on-a-grant-of-representation-pa8b

[82] See chapter on "Useful Addresses"

CHAPTER THIRTEEN

KNOWING WHEN A GRANT HAS BEEN MADE

Obviously, the Personal Representatives will know once a Grant in their favour has been made as they (or their solicitors) will receive the Grant in due course.

Standing Search

There may however be circumstances where another person may wish to know when a Grant has been made. In this case, a standing search should be made instead of lodging a Caveat. A standing search does not prevent the Grant being made and simply informs the applicant when it has been done. This can be useful in circumstances where a person needs to be able to identify the Executors to move forward with a claim, for example, as a creditor of the estate or to lodge a claim under the Inheritance (Provision for Family and Dependants) Act 1975. The standing search will produce a copy of the Grant to the applicant if it is granted within 6 months of the application.

The Standing Search can be obtained using form PA1S[83] and costs £3.

Obtaining a Copy Grant

Where you know that a Grant has been made and simply need one or more copies of it, this can be obtained:

1. Online at https://www.gov.uk/search-will-probate; or

2. By post using Form PA1S.

---

[83] https://assets.publishing.service.gov.uk/government/uploads/system/uploads/attachment_data/file/1001425/PA1S_0721.pdf

Each copy will cost £1.50.

In all cases, the current turnaround time for postal applications is 4 weeks.

CHAPTER FOURTEEN

PROBLEM EXECUTORS

You will from time to time, come across problem Executors. Now I'm not talking about those people who are annoyed that they have not received their inheritance today when Nan was only buried yesterday and are irate that there is a due process to go through (although you will certainly come across a fair few of these people over the course of your career!). In this case, I'm talking about the people who through by accident or design can bring the administration of an estate to a grinding halt.

Where the testator appoints an Executor in the Will, the Executor must do one of the following:

1. Accept their appointment and administer the estate;

2. Have power reserved to them so that while they will not actively administrate the estate at present, they can do so at a future stage if needed; or

3. chose not to act at all, for example, due to ill health or not wishing to be concerned with the responsibility

While a person is free to appoint any executors that they wish in their Will, that freedom to test can raise a number of issues.

<u>Minor Executor</u>

A person under the age of 18 cannot obtain any Grant of Probate/Letters of Administration (with or without Will annexed). This does not negate the minor's appointment as Executor but it does mean that some additional administration is required in order to progress the estate.

Where the minor is the sole Executor, the Grant requires to be taken in the name of an adult residuary beneficiary. Where the minor is the residuary beneficiary, then two people must take the Grant on behalf of the minor, one of whom must be the parent or guardian or the minor. In these cases it will be a Grant *durante minore aetate* that will be taken out by the adult(s).

Once the minor reaches the age of 18 years old, they can then apply for Probate in their own name. This type of Grant is known as a cessate Grant and is a type of double probate. The Grant in the name of the minor now, adult, will supercede the Grant of the previous adult(s).

Unwilling Executors

Whilst you would hope that your testator has alerted their Executors to their appointment ahead of time, there is no requirement to do so. Accordingly, you may find that the appointed Executors do not wish to act (or indeed just do not feel up to the job in the present circumstances).

An appointed Executor can renounce their appointment using form PA15[84]. This means that the Executor gives up all rights to administer the estate.

Where an Executor does not wish to act at present but may wish to act at a later stage, power can be reserved to that Executor. The effect of this is that the person will not act as Executor now but reserves the option to do so in the future.

A spouse/civil partner of the deceased may also renounce their entitlement to obtain letters of administration in an intestate estate but only where there are surviving children or remoter issue of the deceased. This can be done using form PA16[85]. As with testate renunciation, this means that the spouse/civil partner gives up all rights to administer the estate.

---

[84] https://assets.publishing.service.gov.uk/government/uploads/system/uploads/attachment_data/file/990698/PA15_0421_save.pdf

[85] https://assets.publishing.service.gov.uk/government/uploads/system/uploads/attachment_data/file/990707/PA16_0421_save.pdf

In all cases, these forms should be kept safe once executed as they will be needed when the application for a Grant is made.

Mental Incapacitation

A person who is mentally incapable cannot take out a Grant. Form PA14[86] should be completed by a medical professional to confirm the incapacity.

There are a number of options for dealing with this situation:

1. Where the mentally incapable person is appointed alongside one or more other Attorneys, power can be reserved to the incapable person and the Grant taken out in the name of the remaining accepting Executors[87];

2. Where all other possible persons in the same degree as the incapable person have been cleared off, a limited Grant can be made upon instruction from the District Judge or Registrar to:

   a. The person instructed by the Court of Protection to take out the Grant;

   b. Where the Court of Protection is not involved and the mentally incapable person has granted a Power of Attorney (Enduring or Lasting), the Attorney may act on behalf of the incapable adult;

   c. Where none of the foregoing apply or in circumstances where the Attorney renounces the ability to obtain a Grant on behalf of the incapable person, it will be granted in favour of the residuary beneficiary(ies).

Notice must be given of a proposed application in the circumstances laid out at 2.b. and 2.c. above to the Court of Protection. No notice is

---

[86] https://www.gov.uk/government/publications/form-pa14-medical-certificate-probate

[87] R35 Non-Contentious Probate Rules 1987

required in the case of 2.a. as the details of the case will be noted in the original application.

Appointment of a firm

The use of a solicitor as Executor may be of interest to people who expect the proverbial "all hell to break loose" on their death. It is not competent to appoint a firm as Executor but it is competent to appoint some or all members of the firm as Executor. Care needs to be taken as unless the Will expressly refers to the partners/members at the date of death, it will be the relevant partners/members who were in situ in the firm at the date of execution of the Will who will be in the hot seat as Executor. This is not without its difficulties as some or all of those members/partners may have moved firm, retired or died.

Appointment of a Company/Corporate Executor

It is possible to appoint a company as an Executor. How the Grant can be taken out depends on whether the company qualifies as a trust corporation.

A trust corporation can act as Executor, trustee, attorney and/or deputy.[88] The conditions for qualifying for a trust corporation are as follows:

- Must have a place of business in England and Wales;

- Must have the power to undertake Trust services within England and Wales in the Articles of Association; and

- Must have a share capital of at least £250,000, with £100,000 of the share capital paid up (or with an undertaking to pay up upon request in place)

The company may be a trading company (commonly, a bank) or non-trading (for example, a law firm's trustee company).

---

[88] Section 68(18) Trustee Act 1925

Where a trust corporation is appointed, the company can obtain a Grant on their own without the need for an additional Executor.

By comparison, where a company has been appointed and they are not a trust corporation, they cannot take out a Grant[89]. In situations where a company has been appointed, the Grant will be taken out in the name of a director rather than the company. In these circumstances, it will always be Letters of Administration with Will annexed which is granted to the director.

> <u>TIP</u>— Where another solicitor or professional trust company/corporation has been appointed as Executor and it is desired by the beneficiaries/co-Executors that they do not administer the estate, it is a professional courtesy when writing to obtain the professional Executor's declinature, that you give them sufficient information to decline their appointment/acquiesce to a reservation of power. For example, confirm that there are no family disputes which would warrant the continued appointment of an independent party as an Executor or that the estate is a small estate which does not require to go through the Probate process or passes in full to a single beneficiary. Give the professional Executor the reasons why they should not accept their appointment. Do not assume that a professional Executor will automatically resign or reserve power for their appointment. Most corporate Executors will have been appointed for a reason and will wish to consider whether they should act in the administration of the estate. Form PA17 will need to be completed for the professional Executor to step down[90].

<u>Existing Personal Representatives</u>

There may be circumstances where it may be prudent to remove some or all of the Personal Representatives, for example, in situations, where they have failed to progress the administration of the estate. In these cases, the

---

[89] This is different to the position in Scotland, whereby a grant can be taken out in favour of a company.

[90] https://assets.publishing.service.gov.uk/government/uploads/system/uploads/attachment_data/file/990717/PA17_0421_save.pdf

High Court upon due cause being shown may remove one or more of the existing Personal Representatives although it cannot leave the estate without a Personal Representative. In circumstances where all Personal Representatives require to be removed, a substitute will need to be appointed[91].

<u>Disappearance</u>

Where an Executor goes missing or otherwise cannot be found from the outset, you will need to consider whether a tracing agent should be appointed to locate them or, if appropriate, confirm their death in order to progress the estate.

---

[91] S50 Administration of Justice Act 1985. The case of Letterstedt v Broers [1884] UKPC 1 set out the test that the High Court uses when considering whether or not to remove an executor namely "…if satisfied that the continuance of the trustee would prevent the trusts being properly executed, the trustee might be removed. It must always be borne in mind that trustees exist for the benefit of those to whom the creator of the trust has given the trust estate". This can include any nuisance created by the parties, for example, two executors at war who cannot agree on any way forward.

CHAPTER FIFTEEN

INGATHERING ASSETS

Once you have the Grant, you can ingather the assets ready for distribution. This can either be done by transferring the assets directly to the relevant beneficiaries or by encashing the assets. For the purposes of this section, references to Probate also refer to Letters of Administration.

In order to ingather the assets, you will normally need to exhibit the Certificate of Probate along with a completed claim/account closure form or other legal conveyance before you can do so. Asset holders are entitled to ask for Probate where the deceased had in excess of £5,000 of assets with the asset holder[92]. In reality, most asset holders have higher thresholds before insisting on sight of Probate which can be £10,000, £20,000 or in some cases as high as £50,000. This means that you may well be able to get access to funds ahead of Probate or depending on the value and type of assets held, without the need for Probate at all.

Property and land

Property and land can be transferred using usual conveyancing practise. You will need a copy of the title deeds which can usually be found on HM Land Registry[93]. You may need to locate the original title deeds in the event that the property is unregistered. This can be a quite difficult task and should be undertaken as early as possible in proceedings if for no other reason than you do not want to get to the situation where you are going to exchange contracts only to discover that you cannot confirm the ownership trail in the title and lose the sale as a consequence.

---

[92] S1 Administration of Estates (Small Payments) Act 1965

[93] www.gov.uk/get-information-about-property-and-land/search-the-register

A transfer of the full property will involve the use of a TR1 form[94]. A partial transfer will involve the use of a TP1 form[95]. Your conveyancing team will be able to effectively navigate your Executors through the sale or transfer of the property.

Personal Effects

These can either be transferred or sold. In some cases, depending on the nature of the assets (or their age!), any personal effects that are not selected by beneficiaries, will need to simply be disposed of without any benefit, for example, where the furniture does not meet current health and safety standards.

Auction houses can usually either offer house clearance services if the property requires to be cleared or they will be able to advise of local contacts who will offer this service. You may also wish to consider local charities such as the British Heart Foundation or DEFRA who offer house clearance services. However you will be unlikely to receive any money for the items that are taken by the charities and therefore your Executors need to be mindful of their obligation to maximise the estate before choosing a charity to clear the property.

Vehicles

A vehicle can be transferred by signing the transfer slip on the V5. If you do not have the V5 for the vehicle, you will need to obtain a new one from the DVLA before title to the vehicle can be transferred.

If you sell or transfer the vehicle, you will need to apply to have any overpaid vehicle tax to be refunded. The vehicle tax no longer transfers to the new owner. Likewise the new owner will also need to tax the vehicle on transfer to avoid a fine.

---

[94] www.gov.uk/government/publications/registered-titles-whole-transfer-tr1

[95] www.gove.uk/government/publications/registered-titles-part-transfer-tp1

Yachts, Boats and Ships

To transfer the title to a UK registered yacht, boat or ship, the Executors must supply a signed Bill of Sale and register the title with the UK Ship Register. This can be done online[96]. If the yacht, boat or ship is registered abroad, the transfer will need to comply with the registration requirements of the country in which the yacht, boat or ship is registered.

Bank & Building Society accounts

The balances received on closure of bank and building society accounts will almost never be the same value that you were told was in the accounts at date of death. This can be for a variety of reasons such as interest (such as these accounts are currently providing!), credits such as state pension and automated payments such as direct debits and standing orders which have been received/paid post death but prior to the accounts being frozen. The funeral account may also have been settled from the account. If the deceased had debts with the bank/building society such as credit cards or loans, these may also have been settled from the balances on the accounts prior to the funds being sent to you. You should therefore always ask for statements covering the period from date of death to date of closure of the account in order to reconcile the funds received. This will also give you the opportunity to ascertain if there are any other assets that have not otherwise been identified e.g. a standing order crediting from an unknown bank account or a credit from a personal pension.

National Savings & Investments

Premium Bonds can be left in the prize draw for up to a year after the death. There is an option on the encashment form to defer encashment until after the one-year anniversary expires. On the expiry of the one-year anniversary, NSI will automatically redeem the premium bonds and any associated prizes which have been won since the death and remit them by bank or direct transfer where bank account details have been provided or they will issue a cheque.

---

[96] https://www.gov.uk/register-a-boat/the-uk-ship-register

Consideration should be given as to whether savings certificates should be transferred to a beneficiary(ies) or sold. Savings certificates are currently not available to purchase and older certificates in particular gave a decent rate of return which a beneficiary may wish to retain.

All other NS&I assets can be encashed or transferred.

<u>Publicly Listed Shares</u>

Where shares are held by a registrar such as Equiniti, Computershare or Link Asset Services, the registrar will normally offer a postal share dealing service which will enable the shares to be sold or transferred. The forms will normally be sent to you when they reply to your initial enquiry. If the shares are in electronic format, that is to say, you receive a statement rather than a share certificate, you will only need the transfer/sale form with the certificate of Probate to sell/transfer the shares.

If the shares remain in certificated format, you will need the share certificates as well as the certificate of Probate to sell or transfer the shares. In the event that you do not have a share certificate for the full holding, you will need to complete an indemnity which the registrar will provide you with for the missing share certificates. There will be a fee to pay for this service which the Registrar will advise you and which will be payable at the time of lodging the application. The fee will depend on the amount and value of the shares.

Where a postal sale or transfer service is not offered for a listed company, you will need to instruct a stock broker to deal with this matter on your behalf. This is time to make friends with your local friendly broker as not all investment houses will do this for you, particularly if the transaction value is relatively low and there was no previous connection between the deceased and the investment house.

Portfolios of shares managed by a Discretionary Fund Manager (DFM) will be capable of being sold or transferred. Each DFM will have their own way of dealing with taking instructions. Where shares are being transferred to one or more beneficiaries, you may also have to deal with accounts being opened for beneficiaries who do not have an existing account with the DFM.

Private Company Shares

It is common in private companies for there to be restrictions on who can receive shares. There are usually offer round provisions contained in the founding documents of the company. This may mean that before the shares can be transferred tor sold, the shares need to be offered to directors, other shareholders, persons holding a specific office within the company etc. Where those persons fail to take up the shares, the documents may allow for the transfer/sale to follow the terms of the Will or will otherwise detail how the disposal of shares should be dealt with.

These foundation documents can be found on Companies House[97] under Incorporation Documents.

Memorandum of Appropriation

This is a Deed executed by the Executors which transfers assets to a beneficiary and enables the Executor to sell the asset as bare trustees for the beneficiary. This means that any Capital Gains Tax due on the sale of the asset will accrue to the beneficiary and not to the estate. Where there is a large gain, for example on a portfolio of shares, this can reduce the overall amount of tax which would otherwise be payable by the estate were it to sell the asset by enabling the use of multiple Capital Gains Tax allowances from the beneficiaries. In practical terms it enables the Executors to sell the assets as bare trustees for the beneficiaries and therefore any gain arising is payable by the beneficiaries using their own allowances rather than by the estate with its single Capital Gains Tax allowance. It is also useful where assets remain in the estate after 3 tax years and the estate no longer benefits from a Capital Gains Tax allowance to mitigate tax on eventual sale by using the beneficiaries allowances.

---

[97] www.gov.uk/government/organisations/companies-house

Life Policies

Life policies will either be paid immediately upon exhibition of the death certificate or may require a claim form to be completed before the proceeds can be paid. There will usually be an element of interest which is payable on life policies which will be payable on the time between the date of death and date of settlement of the claim. You will need to check whether this interest is paid net or gross of interest and where it has been paid gross of tax, report and pay the Income Tax due on the interest as part of the administration of the estate.

Bonds

Bonds can either be encashed or transferred. If the life assured was the deceased, the bond will come to an end on the notification of the death and the only option will be for the Executors to take the cash.

Ensure your Executors take financial advice before either encashing or transferring a bond that does not terminate on the death of the deceased as a chargeable event may be triggered which will affect either the tax position of the deceased or the estate (depending on timing) and could result in the beneficiaries receiving less than they might otherwise have done had the bond been encashed in a different tax year or transferred to one or more beneficiaries.

State Benefits

Any sums due to the estate from the Department of Work and Pensions will usually be paid direct to a nominated bank account on completion of a form which will be supplied by the Department of Work and Pensions for the Executors to complete.

Personal pensions

Normally death benefits will be payable outwith the estate and will not concern the Executors. There will however be times where there may be some pension which will be payable to the estate, for example, the remainder of a guaranteed annuity or payments due to date of death where payments are made in arrears. This will normally be paid upon completion of a claim form or a letter signed by the Executors directing how the funds should be paid.

HMRC

Any refund of tax that is due to the deceased, will normally be issued by cheque by HMRC made payable to the Executors. They will also pay into an account nominated by the Executors on completion of a self-assessment tax return.

A word of caution though. HMRC's calculations usually do not take account of chargeable events which arise as a consequence of the deceased's death. You may therefore have to go back to HMRC to revise their calculations and possibly repay some or all of any refund received from them.

Refunds

Refunds of other items that have been overpaid, for example Council Tax, energy accounts, credit balances on credit cards etc can either be collected by completion of a claim form or written directions by the Executor to the asset holder on where funds should be paid.

Foreign assets

Foreign assets come with their own unique set of additional requirements to transfer or sell the assets.

Where you have foreign shares, you may have to go through a somewhat torturous process of obtaining a medallion guarantee, particularly for shares held in the USA. A medallion guarantee is a special seal which will enable the foreign registrars to act on the transfer/sale instructions. It effectively is a seal given by a financial institution which guarantees the transaction to the registrars against a fraud. Very few financial institutions within the UK offer this service now. In practical terms, it is most commonly obtained by instructing one of the larger genealogist firms such as Title Research or Fraser & Fraser. You can expect the process of selling/transferring foreign shares to take around 6 months if not longer from start to finish. As soon as you realise that you have foreign assets involved in an estate, it would be advisable to instruct a firm in relation to obtaining the medallion guarantee as there are sometimes tight timescales involved in relation to when documents must be dated from the Court in relation to when the transfer/sale documents are executed to complete the transfer. You will usually require a special extract of the Probate booklet to accompany the transaction documents and therefore it should be ordered at the time of applying for Probate.

You may also have to obtain either a Reseal of Probate or obtain a separate Grant of Probate in the country that holds the foreign asset. In these circumstances, it would be wise to instruct local agents to undertake this work for you. Again, this should be instructed as early as possible into the administration process in order that you have time to ingather or trace relevant documents and understand the time constraints which may apply to overseas procedures.

There is an organisation called The Society of Trusts and Estates Practitioners (STEP). This is a global organisation of solicitors, accountants and financial professionals who specialise in private clients. If you are looking for a foreign contact to instruct, the STEP website has a search facility in which you can locate a relevant professional in a particular country[98]. This should give you a good starting point in instructing someone who knows what they are doing with estate administration in the relevant jurisdiction.

---

[98] https://www.step.org/directory/members

CHAPTER SIXTEEN

PAYMENT OF DEBTS & EXPENSES, DISTRIBUTION & DISCHARGE

Payment of debts and expenses

Before the estate can be distributed to beneficiaries, the outstanding debts of the deceased and the expenses of administration need to be settled from the estate. The funeral expenses, debts and administration expenses of the administration of the estate will be settled from the asset pot in the following order unless there is a contrary provision in the Will which expresses where the settlement of these items should be met from (for example, from a specific asset)[99]:

1. Property of the deceased undisposed of by will, subject to the retention thereof of a fund sufficient to meet any pecuniary legacies;

2. Property of the deceased not specifically devised or bequeathed but included (either by a specific or general description) in a residuary gift, subject to the retention out of such property of a fund sufficient to meet any pecuniary legacies, so far as not provided for as aforesaid;

3. Property of the deceased specifically appropriated or devised or bequeathed (either by a specific or general description) for the payment of debts;

---

[99] Part II Schedule 1 Administration of Estates Act 1925

4. Property of the deceased charged with, or devised or bequeathed (either by a specific or general description) subject to a charge for the payment of debts;

5. The fund, if any, retained to meet pecuniary legacies;

6. Property specifically devised or bequeathed, rateably according to value;

7. Property appointed by will under a general power, including the statutory power to dispose of entailed interests, rateably according to value.

Where all of the above have been exhausted, the Executor can look to property which is not mentioned above such as nominated property or *donatio mortis causa* gifts.

Where an Executor uses property from a later ranking category to settle debts due where there is property from a higher ranking category still available, the beneficiary who has lost out on the assets is entitled to compensation under marshalling principals.

<u>Example</u>

A leaves directions in his Will that a specific gift of shares in ABC Limited is left to B with the residue passing to C. The Executor sells the shares in ABC Limited (category 6) to settle debts due while there are funds comprised in the residue (category 2). B would be entitled to compensation for the shares lost during the administration of the estate.

There is a set order to the settlement of debts and expenses in an estate[100] as follows:

1. Secured debts rank before any other debts and should be paid immediately upon realisation of the asset over which the debt is secured. Where the debt exceeds the value of the asset, the

---

[100] S34(3), S35 and Part II Schedule 1 Administration of Estates Act 1925

balance should be borne from the estate e.g. a mortgage over a property in negative equity;

2. Reasonable funeral and testamentary debts;

3. Specially preferred debts

4. Preferential debts

    o   Arrears of state and occupational pension contributions

    o   Salary and holiday pay owed to employees of the deceased

5. Ordinary debts – all other debts other than the aforementioned

6. Interest due on preferential and ordinary debts

7. Deferred debts

When dealing with a category, all creditors within that category rank equally. This means that you must pay all debts in that category in full or if you have insufficient funds to do so, the debts should be paid pro rata. You cannot pay one or some debts in full but partially pay the other creditors in the category or not at all. Where this principal is not followed or if the debts are paid out of order, the Executor can find themselves personally liable for paying the outstanding higher ranking debts – needless to say, not a position that either you or your client would want to be in!

Order of Settlement of the Estate

The Executors would be well advised not to distribute the estate until s27 Trustee Act 1925 adverts have been placed and expired in case an otherwise unknown creditor comes to light. If this is the case and the Executors have already distributed the estate within that time frame, they will become personally liable to settle the debt.

Once the debts and expenses of the estate have been settled, you can then look to settle the estate with the beneficiaries. Again, there is a set order for the settlement of the estate with beneficiaries as follows:

1. Specific Legacies;

2. General Legacies;

3. Residue – this is a share of the residue of the estate, that is to say, everything that is left over after settlement of all debts, funeral expenses, taxes, legacies and administration expenses of the estate.

Legacies are payable out of undisposed of property first and thereafter out of the residue unless there is a contrary intention shown in the Will.

Specific legacies

These are legacies of things such as a clock, Nan's engagement ring etc.

Where the asset referred to in the Will cannot be found or is no longer owned by the deceased at the time of their death, the legacy will fail unless there is a contra indication in the Will that the beneficiary should receive some other item or share of the estate.

Specific legacies can be tricky where care has not been taken to sufficiently identify the item in question in the Will or where the deceased had multiple items which could fit the description.

TIP – when drafting specific legacies in Wills, try to make the description sufficiently clear to enable identification of the item on death. If at all possible, get a photo of the item that can have the description of the item written on the back of it and stored with the Will to aid identification e.g. this is the diamond ring being left to my niece, Josephine Bloggs under the terms of Clause 4f of my Will dated 3 April 2017

A receipt from the beneficiary to acknowledge receipt should be sufficient discharge to the Executors in the exercise of their duties.

General legacies

These are usually cash legacies (also referred to as pecuniary legacies). They can however include demonstrative legacies. Demonstrative legacies are a direction to the Executor to acquire a particular item for a beneficiary and are usually identified by the notable absence of the use of the word "my" e.g. I leave 1,000 shares in Lloyds Banking Group PLC.

Example

The Will says "I leave my shares in Lloyds Banking Group PLC to A", then A will either receive all of the shares if they are still comprised in the estate at date of death or a lesser amount if the abatement rules apply.

Where the Will says " I leave 1,000 shares in Lloyds Banking Group PLC to A" and no such shares are comprised within the estate then the Executors must purchase this item for the beneficiary.

Needless to say, if you are involved in drafting Wills, you want to make sure that you do not inadvertently include demonstrative legacies by your terminology or if using these types of legacies deliberately, that they are indeed attainable by the estate – that is to say, don't go leaving a legacy of the Mona Lisa to anyone!

Interest on General Legacies

Where the pecuniary legacy is paid within one year of death, no interest is payable unless a contrary expression is contained in the Will. Otherwise if the legacy is paid after the first year anniversary, interest runs at the statutory rate from the one year anniversary to the date of payment on a non-compounded basis. Where there is a contingent legacy e.g. I leave £10,000 to A upon her attaining 21 years old, interest will only run from the date of the 21st birthday until payment (assuming that the contingency occurs after the one-year anniversary of the death – if it arises before, the usual one year rule applies and no interest will be paid until the one year anniversary of the death is reached).

If the legacy is to a child of the deceased or a person to whom the deceased stood *in loco parentis*, interest runs from the date of death.

Where the legacy is free of Inheritance Tax, the interest will apply to the full value of the legacy. Where there is a direction that the legacy is subject to tax, interest will only apply to the net value of the legacy after Inheritance Tax has been deducted.

Residue

This covers the pot of assets that is left after settlement of all debts, funeral expenses, taxes, legacies and administration expenses.

Abatement

Where there are insufficient assets to settle legacies in full, the legacies will abate pro rata. The order of abatement is as follows[101]:

1. Residue

2. General legacies (including demonstrative legacies)

3. Specific legacies

Example

A dies leaving an estate worth £10,000 with debts, funeral expenses and administration expenses of £7,500. This leaves a net estate of £2,500.

Under the terms of A's Will, they left legacies of £2,000 each to B and C.

The estate does not have £4,000 to settle the legacies in full to each of B and C.

In this case, as the legacies are of equal amounts B and C will each receive £1,250 each and the legacies will exhaust the estate with the residuary beneficiaries receiving nothing.

---

[101] Part II Schedule 1 Administration of Estates Act 1925

Example

A dies leaving an estate per the terms of the example above.

Under the terms of A's Will this time, they left legacies of £1,000 to B and £3,000 to C.

Again, the estate does not have £4,000 to settle the legacies in full to each of B and C.

In this case, the legatees will receive the following:

B = £1,000 (legacy)

-------------------- x £2,500 (free estate) = £625 (abated legacy to B)

(£1,000 + £3,000) (total legacies)

C = £3,000 (legacy)

------------------ x £2,500 (free estate) = £1,875 (abated legacy to C)

(£1,000 + £3,000) (total legacies)

Again, the residuary beneficiaries will receive nothing from the estate as the legacies have exhausted the estate.

Ademption

This occurs where a specific legacy referred to in the Will no longer exists at the time of the death. In this situation, the legatee will not receive anything in satisfaction of their legacy from the estate. This can however be overridden by a contrary term in the Will e.g. I direct my Executors to make over my shares in ABC Limited or the sale proceeds thereof held at my death[102]. In this situation, the legatee would receive the proceeds received from sale held within the estate.

---

[102] Re Lewis's WT (1937) Ch 118

Transfer of Assets

Where the beneficiaries would wish assets transferred to them in lieu of them being sold and there is insufficient cash within the estate to meet all of the debts, taxes and expenses of administration of the estate, it will be necessary for the beneficiary to introduce the shortfall caused by them choosing to acquire the asset rather than having it sold prior to the transfers of assets being undertaken.

Purchase of Assets by a Beneficiary

It is possible for a beneficiary to purchase an asset from the estate. Most commonly, offers to purchase assets will be in relation to the house of the deceased. The Executors are under a duty to maximise the value of the estate for the beneficiaries. In circumstances where an offer to purchase an asset from a beneficiary is received, you will need to consider the pros and cons of the acceptance of the offer versus putting the property on the open market and seeing what offers are received.

You may find that the family are more than happy to receive an offer from a beneficiary at the date of death value or an enhanced value without placing the property on the market as this will save the estate the estate agency and marketing costs to sell the assets. They will also have some degree of certainty that the transaction will not fall through due to lack of funding thus avoiding incurring aborted sale fees.

Where there is any sort of dispute as to the sale price (or indeed which beneficiary should have the opportunity to purchase the property), the Executors should consider an open market sale where the beneficiary so wishing to acquire the property can have the opportunity to bid for the property and take their chances in the open market. Ultimately it will be for the Executors to decide which offer is accepted. In these circumstances, they may not select the highest offer because a lower offer is a cash purchase compared to a mortgaged purchase or because the purchaser isn't caught in a chain.

Where a beneficiary is entitled to a share of the residue which comprises the asset in question, they will not need to introduce the full sale price into the estate to acquire the asset – they will only require to introduce the difference between their share of the asset and the sale price.

Example

A is entitled to a one quarter share of the residue of the estate which comprises a property worth £200,000.

A wishes to purchase the property from the estate and a sale price is agreed at £240,000.

A will only need to introduce £180,000 to acquire the property (three quarters of the sale price) as they are already entitled to one quarter of the value of the asset.

Accounts

It will be necessary to prepare account of the intromissions of the Executors for approval. There is a school of thought that suggests that accounts should be prepared at the end of the estate once everything has been ingathered. I prefer to draft the accounts as I am going along for the following reasons:

1. The capital and debts schedules detailing the assets at date of death can be used to form the basis of the assessment for Inheritance Tax purposes;

2. You can see problems in cash flow before they arise either for settlement of debts, expenses and taxes or in terms of whether assets should be transferred to beneficiaries or be sold;

3. You can see what income has arisen in the tax year to be able to prepare R185es;

4. You can see whether you have a Capital Gains Tax issue and either take action to reduce the gain or register the estate in time to prepare self-assessment returns.

These accounts should detail the following:

1. Assets at date of death

2. Additional estate found post Confirmation

3. Sundry receipts

4. Income

5. Legacies

6. Expenses of administration

7. Division of the residue

There are various types of accounts that can be prepared as follows:

1. Statement of receipt and payments

2. Charge and discharge account

3. Schedular account

The choice is yours as to which style of accounting will be most suitable for your practice or estate. There is really no right or wrong option although I have provided my thoughts below on when each type of account may be suitable depending on what has happened in the estate.

<u>Statement of Receipts and Payments</u>

This is (in my humble opinion) really only suitable for very small estates where there are only a few transactions. This type of account consists of three sections:

1. Credits

2. Debits

3. Division of residue

It is basically a replication of the credits and debits from your cash ledger.

It will not help you identify whether there is any tax to pay for the period of administration of the estate.

Account of Charge and Discharge

This might be considered to be the traditional way of preparing accounts for an estate and is a step further than the statement of receipts and payments.

It is effectively a summary of all credit and debits and ensures that the credit side equals the debit side.

As it summarises everything into categories again it will not easily help you identify whether there is any tax to pay for the period of administration of the estate.

Schedular account

I find that this account is the easiest account style to use to ensure that you don't miss anything tax wise during the administration of the estate. It sets out each individual component of the estate on a separate page thus making it easier to ascertain if an Income Tax liability has arisen and in what tax year and also whether Capital Gains Tax will be an issue. It will also help you identify if a beneficiary needs to introduce funds into the estate to balance off their share of their estate and expenses of administration.

It can also be expanded to include Schemes of Division and personal statements where assets have been sold as bare trustees following a Memorandum of Appropriation being entered into.

Discharge

Once the accounts have been prepared, they should be sent to the Executor(s) for approval prior to final distribution to the beneficiaries. It is competent to either have all Executors sign a single set of accounts or have each Executor sign an individual set of accounts and keep all signed copies together in the executry records.

Once the Executors have approved the accounts, a copy should be circulated to the residuary beneficiaries to approve and discharge the Executor of their duties before final payment is made.

Where there is power in the Will to pay to a minor or guardian or any other person having control over someone who lacks legal capacity, the discharge should be modified to include the capacity in which the person is signing e.g. as parent, guardian, deputy etc of the beneficiary and an indemnity to the Executor in the event that the parent spends the legacy on themselves or on A N other rather than on the legatee themselves and the legatee decides to sue the Executor for negligence In these circumstances, it may well be worth running a check on the Land Register for the parent to ascertain if they have a previous history of bankruptcy before making payment[103].

---

[103] https://www.gov.uk/guidance/land-registry-portal-how-to-make-a-bankruptcy-search

CHAPTER SEVENTEEN

VARYING THE TERMS
OF AN ESTATE

It is possible to redirect an entitlement from an estate. This may be because:

- a beneficiary doesn't need or want all of their entitlement;

- to honour wishes of the testator which were made known to the beneficiaries before the death but to which the testator had not been able to commit to writing before the death; or

- to rectify a perceived "wrong" in the Will.

It does not matter whether the deceased died testate or intestate.

A redirection of some or all of the estate can occur within or outwith the estate.

Gifts

The intended recipient (the donor) of the share of the estate can simply gift their entitlement (or whatever part they wish to dispose of) to the new recipient. If this is done, this will be a Potentially Exempt Transfer (PET) and the donor will require to survive the transfer by 7 years for it to fall outwith their estate for Inheritance Tax purposes.

This would normally be used in situations where more than 2 years have elapsed between the date of death and the transfer of property is taking place. It can also be used where the value of the transfer to the new beneficiary(ies) is already covered by one or more of the gifting exemptions (see the Inheritance Tax chapter of this book for further information).

Deed of Variation

An alternative to gifts is to enter into a Deed of Variation (also known as a Deed of Family Arrangement). A Deed of Variation can be entered into in respect of a testate or intestate estate. A Deed of Variation is a formal written deed which has the effect of rewriting the terms of the Will or the intestacy to redirect the donor's share of the estate (or part share or a specific asset as the case may be) to the new beneficiary or beneficiaries.

The conditions for a Deed of Variation to work are as follows:

1. It must be entered into within 2 years of the date of death;

2. It must be in writing;

3. It must contain a declaration that the Deed is to be treated as a variation under s142 Inheritance Tax Act 1984;

4. It must be signed by the donor;

5. It must not be made in exchange for any goods or benefits, for example entering into a Deed of Variation to give someone benefit in exchange for a return of cash;

6. Where the variation is in favour of a charity or registered club, that charity or club has been given notice of the variation; and

7. In situations where the terms of the Deed alters the Inheritance Tax treatment of the estate, it must be intimated to HMRC and any additional Inheritance Tax due must be paid along with interest (if appropriate)

Charities

Where a variation is in favour of a charity or registered club, the easiest way to prove that they have received notification of the variation is to have them counter sign the Deed. Where there are multiple parties, you might not want to risk circulating the principal deed and therefore you can show that you have intimated the Deed on the relevant parties by providing a copy of the letter sent to the parties to advise. These letters can be sent by recorded delivery and the delivery numbers provided as well to enable HMRC to look up the Royal Mail website to check that delivery has taken place.

Timescales

A Deed of Variation can be undertaken at any time in the two-year period from the date of death and will apply regardless of whether the assets remain unadministered within the estate or have been distributed in full or in part to the donor.

An important point to note is that a variation can only be undertaken once – it is therefore important that you get the terms correct and it is undertaken on time as it cannot be redone.

Effect

Another important point to note is that the Deed of Variation only works for Inheritance Tax and succession law purposes. For Capital Gains Tax and Income Tax purposes, liability for any such tax due on the varied estates remains with the donor. It can also be viewed as a voluntary divestment of assets by the donor for the purposes of assessment of care costs and other means tested benefits should the donor require a financial assessment or already be within the care regime.

Pitfall for the Unwary

All parties affected by the Deed of Variation must be capable of consenting to the variation. Minors and adults lacking capacity can prove to be problematic when it comes to varying an estate as they will be unable to consent to a variation of their share of the estate. This will not prohibit anyone else from varying their own individual share of the estate but can affect the ability to vary where the benefit is, for example, held jointly with a person who lacks capacity or where there is a trust which needs varied but involves one or more persons who lack capacity. Where a variation is not possible, and one party still wishes to divest themselves of the asset, they are of course free to decline their share of the estate, assign their share or alternatively, receive the share of the estate and then gift it on (however the 7-year PET rules will apply rather than the preferential treatment of the variation which bypasses their estate completely).

Disclaimers

This is most likely to occur where there has been a family fall out and the intended beneficiary wants nothing from the deceased's estate. This is not however the only situation in which this can occur.

A person may disclaim their entitlement from the estate either in writing or orally. A disclaimer in writing is preferable if for no other reason than the Executors can prove in the event of a later dispute that they acted in a fitting manner.

An effective disclaimer must:-

1. disclaim all of the benefit left to the beneficiary. If only part of a benefit needs to be redirected, then a Deed of Variation would be the most appropriate mechanism to deploy;

2. the claimant cannot have derived any benefit from their share of the estate at the time the disclaimer is made;

3. the claimant cannot direct who should receive their share of the estate in substitution. Again, if the claimant wishes to control who inherits their share of the estate, a Deed of Variation would be the most appropriate mechanism;

4. where Tax benefits are sought, the disclaimer must be in writing.

It is possible for any disclaimer to be retracted however this can only occur where no one else has acted to their detriment following the disclaiming of the share of the estate. The fact that a disclaimer can be retracted illustrates further why it is best practice to get any disclaim of benefit committed to writing as then the Executors can prove the effective date for when the disclaim happened and can establish who has taken what action and the ramifications of it for all beneficiaries of the estate should the disclaimer change their mind at a later stage.

Differences between Deeds of Variation and Disclaimers

Disclaimer	Deed of Variation
Declines all benefit from the estate	Accepts the benefit from the estate then redirects some or all of it
Ineffective where a benefit has been derived from the share of the estate.	Can take effect regardless of whether a benefit has already been derived from the share of the estate.
Cannot direct who should benefit in substitution for the Disclaimer.	Can direct who should receive the varied entitlement and in what proportions.
A disclaimer can be made at any time as long as the conditions are met.	Must take effect within two years of the date of death to be effective for Tax purposes.
Can be done orally or in writing.	Must be in writing only.
Qualifies for Section 142 (1) Inheritance Tax Act 1984 and Section 62 (6) Taxation Capital Gains Act 1992 relief but only when committed to writing.	Qualifies for Section 142 (1) Inheritance Tax Act 1984 and Section 62 (6) Taxation Capital Gains Act 1992 relief.

Mutual Wills

Mutual Wills are Wills where a couple are bound to the terms of the Wills as executed and changes cannot be made without the consent of the other party. They are not to be confused with Mirror Wills where the wills for a couple are drafted in mirror terms but the testators are free to change their Wills as and when they feel fit.

Where there is a mutual Will in place, all testators agree to be bound by the terms of the Wills which are drafted in mirror terms and will not revoke the wills following the death of the first to die. The effect of this is that the first death acts like a barrier to prevent the surviving testator(s) from changing their Will(s). Essentially, the succession to the survivor's estate is stuck with the provisions contained in the mutual Will. You may find this in situations where it is a second or subsequent marriage/civil partnership or relationship where provision has been made for children of a previous marriage and the testators do not wish such provision to be changed (effectively to prevent sideways disinheritance of children on a subsequent marriage of the survivor).

CHAPTER EIGHTEEN

INHERITANCE TAX

This is the tax that is guaranteed to send both clients and practitioners around the bend! This book will only scratch the surface of what you will come across on the Inheritance Tax (IHT) arena but it should at least give you the basics to get to grips with the most frequent IHT issues that you are likely to come across. For a more thorough in depth look at IHT, look at Tolley's Inheritance Tax by Malcolm Gunn[104].

The Basics

The point at which IHT usually (key word here is usually!) becomes payable is when an estate exceeds the nil rate band (NRB) as set from time to time. The NRB at the time of writing this book[105] is £325,000. It has remained static since 2009 and is not expected to rise before 2028. Estate above that limit is subject to IHT at 40% unless there is an exemption or relief which applies. This should be your starting point for all estate transactions.

The Transferable Nil Rate Band

This applies to married couples and enables the unused portion of the first to die's NRB to be transferred to the second to die's estate to offset IHT on the second death.

Residential Enhancement to the NRB

The Residential Enhancement to the NRB or Residence Nil Rate Band (RNRB or RENRB for short) was introduced to extend the NRB where a qualifying residential interest is passed to lineal descendants on a death.

---

[104] This publication is updated annually.

[105] December 2022

It does not apply to Potentially Exempt Transfers (successful or failed) or Chargeable Lifetime Transfers. It only applies to the IHT due on estate assets.

A qualifying residential interest is an interest in a dwelling house which has been the deceased's residence. If the deceased owns two or more residential dwelling house interests at death, their Executors may elect only one to become the qualifying residential interest. Confusingly, the legislation was extended to enable the RNRB to be used where the deceased had owned a property at some point in their lives but no longer owned a property at the time of their death – for example, because they had moved into permanent residential care and their house had been sold to fund their care. This means that where the latter situation applies, you will need to track down records of the disposal to be able to calculate the application of the RNRB to the estate.

Lineal descendants for the purposes of RNRB are classed as:

1. Children of the deceased;

2. Adopted children of the deceased;

3. Foster children of the deceased;

4. Any child to whom the deceased was appointed as a Guardian; and

5. Children and remoter issue of any of the above categories

You will notice that this includes categories of person who do not normally get a look in for succession law purposes or indeed for any other familial IHT exemption.

The RNRB, much like the NRB, is capable of revision by Parliament. Unlike the NRB, it has moved several times since 2017 as follows:

1. For deaths on or after 6 April 2017 – £100,000

2. For deaths occurring in the tax year 2018/19 – £125,000

3. For deaths occurring in the tax year 2019/20 – £150,000

4. For deaths occurring on or after 6 April 2020 – £175,000

The RNRB only applies to estates under £2m. It tapers off up to estates over £2.2m. Estates above £2.2m do not qualify for the relief.

While normally there must be a gift of the qualifying residential interest to a lineal descendant outright for the Residential Enhancement, it will also apply where the lineal descendant is a beneficiary of a trust set up on the death of the deceased which falls into one of the following categories and of which the qualifying residential interest is an asset:

1. Immediate post death interest in possession trust (IPDI);

2. Disabled persons trust;

3. Trust for bereaved minors; or

4. 18-25 Trusts

It is important to note that a disposal into a discretionary trust on death will **not** apply to benefit from the RNRB. This is a particularly important as a significant number of older Wills still carry a discretionary nil rate band trust clause within them. This was a tax planning mechanism deployed before the advent of the transferable nil rate band which enabled the nil rate band of the first spouse to die to be utilised in full or in part in situations where it would otherwise have been lost by passing the estate in full to the surviving spouse.

Unlike many other IHT reliefs and exemptions, you do not need to be married to take advantage of this relief but you do need to have a qualifying lineal descendent and either have a qualifying property or qualify under the downsizing rules.

TIP – It is well worth reviewing your Will bank every 3 years or so. This will enable you to remind clients that they have made a Will (with you!). It also allows outdated tax planning in Wills to be revised as well as ensuring that the client's Will remains up to date taking account of their family circumstances.

The Transferable RNRB

As with the TNRB, the balance of unused RNRB is transferable to the estate of the surviving spouse or civil partner. Where the first death occurs prior to 6 April 2017, you can still transfer their allowance even though it did not apply at the time of their death. It can also apply where the property the transferable RNRB (TRNRB) applies to is not the same property that the first to die and the current deceased resided in together. As the first to die could not have used any of their RNRB if they died before 6 April 2017, 100% of their RNRB will be available to transfer to the survivor.

The TRNRB is based on a percentage basis. This means that you will need to calculate the unused portion of the first to die's RNRB. This is done as follows:

Unused portion of the first to die's RNRB

_____ X 100%

The RNRB applicable at the date of the first to die's death

You then multiply that percentage by the applicable RNRB at the time of the second to die's death and that will give you the available TRNRB.

It is worth noting that the maximum TRNRB is 100%. This means that if the deceased has been widowed twice, their executors can only claim TRNRB up to 100% of the value of the RNRB applicable at the time of the second to die.

Example

A marries B in 2002. B dies in 2005.

A marries C in 2009. C dies in 2016

A dies in 2021 when the RNRB is £175,000.

A's Executors wish to claim the TRNRB.

As both B and C died before 6 April 2017, 100% of their RNRB is available to transfer to A's estate.

A's Executor's can only claim £175,000 as the TRNRB. They can choose whether to use B or C's estate to transfer the RNRB.

Example

A marries B in April 2018. B dies in January 2019. B's executors used 75% of his RNRB.

A marries C in December 2019. C dies in May 2020. C's Executors used 25% of his RNRB.

A dies in 2021 when the RNRB is £175,000.

A's Executors wish to claim the TRNRB.

A's Executors can claim 25% of the unused TRNRB from B's estate (100% - 75% used on B's death) and 75% of the unused TRNRB from C's estate (100% - 25% used on C's death) thus enabling A's Executors to claim 100% TRNRB.

Had B's Executors used 90% of his RNRB, then A's Executors would only be able to claim 10% TRNRB from B's estate which when combined with the 75% available from C's estate would give A's Executors a maximum claim to the TRNRB of 85%

What is subject to IHT?

Once your initial investigations are complete, you will have ascertained the value of the estate. In addition, you will need to ascertain what gifts the deceased made in the 7 years preceding the death (and in some cases the 14 years preceding death but more of that later!) as these can affect the total IHT which will be payable by the estate. It is important that questions regarding gifts are asked of Executors and close family as HMRC can charge up to 100% of the tax due on non-declared gifts as a penalty in addition to the actual tax that falls due[106]. It is also worth looking at bank statements to see if you can identify any gifts. Standing orders to family members will normally be at least indicative of a gift with the onus on the recipient to prove it was not a gift e.g. they can prove its payment for a subscription for the deceased, weekly shopping for the deceased etc. Cheques can also be another source of gifts. You can ask the bank to provide copies of the fronts of cheques that you suspect may be gifts.

There are different types of gifts that you need to be aware of when looking at estates. For these purposes, a gift can be anything. It can be cash, property, investments, jewellery and other personal effects or even a share in a business. The person gifting the asset is known as the donor and the person receiving the gift is known as the donee.

Particular care needs to be given where assets are sold at undervalue in a non-arm's length transaction as the difference between the sale price and the market value of the asset will also be classed as a gift.

---

[106] Hutchings V HMRC [2015] UKFTT 9 (TC) – case in which HMRC discovered a significant gift made by the deceased to his son through an offshore account via an anonymous tip off which the son had failed to declare to the solicitors handling the estate. The tax assessed as due on the gift was over £100,000 for which a penalty of 50% of the tax due was applied. The son appealed the decision blaming grief for forgetting about the gift. Had the Executors not written the letter, it is likely that the Executors would have been found personally liable for the penalty and the solicitors advising the Executors would have been looking at a negligence claim.

Example

A owns a house. A wishes to downsize and their child B wishes to get a foot on the property ladder. A sells the house off market to B for £300,000. The actual open market value of the property at the time of sale is worth £400,000. Regardless of the fact that A has received cash in exchange for the asset, the gift element of the transaction is the £100,000 discount on the sale price.

As IHT is not straightforward, there are different types of gifts that you can come across when dealing with an estate.

Potentially Exempt Transfer otherwise known as a PET

PETs are gifts made to an individual. PETs are exempt from IHT regardless of value **if** the person making the gift survives the date of gift by 7 years. Note that the 7-year clock for gifts does not start until the funds or asset have left the donor so the clock for gifts made by cheque will not start ticking until the recipient has banked the cheque and it has cleared the donor's account or the asset e.g. a painting, jewellery etc has left the possession of the donor.

Failed Potentially Exempt Transfer otherwise known as a Failed PET

This is where the donor fails to survive the gift by 7 years. In this case, the failed PETs have the first bite of the cherry so to speak in respect of the NRB applicable at the time of the deceased's death which can alter the ultimate division of the estate.

Example

Mrs A makes the following capital gifts:

- £100,000 to her niece Miss B on 25 September 2020

- £50,000 to her nephew Mr C on 6 April 2019

- £25,000 to her goddaughter, Ms D on 12 May 2002

Mrs A dies on 30 June 2021 with a nil rate band of £325,000 to offset the tax due on her estate.

You need to look back the 7 years from the date of death to 30 June 2014 to capture any gifts made.

In this case the gifts to Miss B and Mr C are caught within the 7-year timeframe preceding the date of death.

Accordingly, the nil rate band available to offset IHT against the estate assets is £175,000 namely £325,000 - £100,000 (Miss B gift) - £50,000 (Mr C).

The gift to Ms D was made too far back in time to be brought into account.

<u>Example</u>

Say Mrs A's Will leaves her estate equally between her sister's children, Miss E, Miss F and Mr H and her net estate at the date of death is £400,000. The balance of the estate which is subject to IHT is £75,000 (£400,000 - £325,000 NRB) and the IHT thereon is £30,000 (£75,000 x 40%). Administration expenses are £10,000. This means that each beneficiary will receive £120,000 each (namely (£400,000 - £30,000 IHT - £10,000 expenses)/3).

However, when taking account of the gifts in the first example, the residue of the estate changes so that each beneficiary will receive £100,000. This is calculated by:

Net estate at date of death = £400,000

Available NRB to offset against estate at date of death = £325,000 - £100,000 Miss B gift - £50,000 Mr C gift = £175,000

Estate subject to IHT = £400,000 (net estate) - £175,000 (available NRB) = £225,000.

Tax due on estate = £225,000 (estate subject to IHT) x 40% = £90,000

Residuary estate = £400,000 (net estate) - £90,000 (IHT) - £10,000 (administration expenses) = £300,000

Each beneficiary receives £100,000 (residuary estate/3)

As you will see, the failed PETs have significantly reduced the amounts the residuary beneficiaries will receive from the estate.

Lifetime Gifts

Exempt Gifts

These are gifts that are exempt from IHT. There are different categories of exempt gifts as follows:

- Transfers between spouses/civil partners – these are free of IHT regardless of whether the transfer is 1p or £100m. To take advantage of this exemption, the spouse/civil partner must live permanently in the UK and be legally married or in a civil partnership with the donor. If either of these conditions are not met, then any benefit derived by the spouse will be treated as if the spouse is a non-exempt beneficiary.

- Annual exemption – each person has a £3,000 annual exemption which they can use to make gifts which will be free of IHT. This can either be a single transaction up to £3,000 or can be comprised of a series of smaller transactions up to that value. It can also be used as a part exemption against larger gifts. If an annual allowance has not been utilised, it can be carried forward to the following year but the annual allowance for that tax year must be utilised first before the carried forward allowance can be used. You can only carry forward one year's unused annual allowance.

<u>Example</u>

A makes a gift of £10,000 to their friend B. A has made no other gifts during the current tax year. The tax treatment of the £10,000 gift will be £3,000 being exempt under the annual allowance and the £7,000 being a PET which requires to be survived by the donor by 7 years to fall out with the donor's estate.

<u>Example</u>

A makes a gift of £10,000 to their friend B. A has made no other gifts during the current tax year. A also made no gifts during the immediately preceding tax year. The tax treatment of the £10,000 gift will be £3,000 being exempt under the current year's annual allowance, a further £3,000 being exempt under the previous year's annual allowance and the £4,000 balance being a PET which requires to be survived by the donor by 7 years to fall out with the donor's estate.

<u>Small gifts</u>

You can make any number of gifts to any number of individuals up to the total value of £250 per recipient in any tax year and it will be free of IHT. The condition is that the **total** of the gifts to any **one person** must **not** exceed £250 **in a single tax year**. If the total gift(s) does exceed £250, then you need to look at whether the annual allowance will apply in full or in part to the gift and where it doesn't apply, the balance will be a PET.

<u>Example</u>

A makes the following gifts during tax year 2020/2021:

- B – £95

- C – £105 and £54

- D – £56 and £100

- E – £145

As the total of all gifts made by A to each beneficiary are under £250 within the relevant tax year, each gift falls within the small gifts exemption and are exempt from IHT.

Example

A makes the following gifts during tax year 2020/2021:

- B – £95

- C – £205 and £54

- D – £56 and £100

- E – £145 and £110

In this situation, only the gifts to B and D would fall within the small gifts exemption. The gifts to C and E do not qualify for the small gifts exemption as they total in excess of £250 to each beneficiary. In this case, the gifts to C and E will take up £259 and £255 respectively from A's annual allowance.

Gifts to UK charities

Gifts to UK charities are exempt from IHT. The charity must be registered within the UK to qualify. Foreign charities do not qualify for this exemption and gifts to foreign charities will be PETs or Failed PETs as the case may be.

Gifts to UK political parties[107]

These types of gifts are exempt from IHT although gifts to national parties over £7,500 must be declared publicly as must gifts over £1,500 to local associations. In order to qualify, the party being donated to must have had at the last election:

---

[107] S24 IHTA 1984

1. at least 2 MPs voted in; or

2. One MP voted in with 150,000 votes[108].

If the party does not meet either criteria then the gift will be classed as PET or Failed PET.

<u>Gifts on marriage</u>

The amount of a gift that will be exempt on marriage depends on the relationship of the recipient to the donor. Gifts of up to £5,000 in favour of a child will be exempt. This amount reduces to £2,500 where the recipient is a grandchild of the donor and reduces further to £1,000 to anyone else (including your fiancé/fiancée!). For this exemption to work, the gift must be given in contemplation of a specific marriage and the marriage must take place. It is not sufficient to give a gift in contemplation that the person may one day get married.

<u>When is a PET not a PET?</u>

Another trap for the unwary in identifying gifts is in situations where the deceased has given away an asset but still retains a benefit. This is known as a gift with reservation of benefit (GWR, GWRB or GWROB for short). In this situation, the 7 year PET clock does not start ticking until the donor ceases to have a benefit from the gift. The most common situation where you will come across this is where the deceased owned a property and then gifted it to one or more of their children during their lifetime but continued to live in the property. In this case, the value of the gift is the value of the asset at the time the deceased ceased to have a benefit from the asset rather than the value at the date of the gift.

<u>Example</u>

A owns a property worth £200,000. A gifts the property to their children B and C on 1 July 2007. A continues to reside in the property until their death on 31 December 2017. At the time of A's death, the property was

---

[108] Banks V HMRC, 2018 UKFTT 617 TC

worth £250,000. The value of the gift brought back into account for the estate is £250,000.

Example

A owns a property worth £300,000. A gifts the property to their child B on 21 August 2003. A continues to reside in the property until A moved into permanent residential care death on 14 February 2016 at which point B moves into the property. A dies on 31 June 2019. At the time that A moved into permanent residential care the property was worth £390,000 and at the time of their death, the property was worth £425,000. The gift became a PET on 14 February 2016 as the deceased received no further benefit from the asset and the value attributable to the gift is £390,000

A GWROB can be avoided by the donor paying an open market rental for the use of the asset. This is known as a pre-owned asset tax or POAT for short. By paying for the use of the asset, it allows the usual 7 year clock to start ticking immediately to lift the asset out of your estate. The conditions to meet the pre owned asset tax rules are that:

1. You must pay an open market rent for the use of the asset;

2. The asset needs to be valued every 5 years where the POAT charge is in place to ensure that a fair market rent continues to be paid;

3. Where a full market value rent is paid for the asset, the Inheritance Tax charge will not apply;

4. POAT is a charge to Income Tax rather than IHT despite its application in respect of the operation of gifts.

Chargeable Lifetime Transfer otherwise known as a CLT

This is a gift which unlike a PET is immediately subject to an IHT charge. This will occur where the donor makes a settlement into a relevant property trust (RPT) which when added together with all other CLTs made in the 7 years prior to this settlement exceed the nil rate band. Unlike regular gifts, the IHT charge is levied at 20% rather than the estate rate of 40%. If the donor dies within 7 years of the CLT, a further 20% becomes chargeable on the gift bringing it up to the estate rate of 40%.

The backwards shadow

This is where the gifts in the 14 years prior to death rule comes in. It will apply where a PET fails in the 7 years prior to death. In that case, it is necessary to then look at the gifts that have been made in the 7 years prior to the PET that failed. Where there have been CLT's made in the 7 years prior to the failed PET, these will require to be taken into account when calculating the IHT due in connection with the estate.

Example

A settles £275,000 into a discretionary trust on 4 July 2008. A had not made any gifts of any description prior to this settlement. This is a CLT but as it is under the applicable NRB at the time of settlement, there is no IHT to pay on the settlement into the trust.

A then gifts cash to his god daughter B of £500,000 on 4 January 2014. This is a PET. There will be no IHT due on the occasion of this gift and will fall out with A's estate if A survives until 4 January 2021.

The CLT will only affect the PET if A fails to survive until 4 January 2021.

A dies on 14 February 2020. A's net estate at date of death is worth £400,000. The NRB at the time of A's death is £325,000.

The treatment of the CLT and the PET are as follows:

The CLT uses the first £275,000 of the NRB leaving £50,000 of the NRB available.

The next claim on the NRB is the now failed PET. £50,000 is deducted from the value of the PET leaving £450,000 of the failed PET chargeable to IHT at 40%. Taper Relief will apply to reduce the effective rate of

IHT due on the failed PET as the failed PET was made between 3-7 years before A's death (see below for further information).

There is no NRB available to offset any IHT in the estate assets and therefore the full £400,000 of estate is subject to IHT at 40%.

Had A died on 30 July 2021, the PET would not have failed and would have been out with the 7 years of the date of death. As such, it would not be counted for IHT purposes. As the PET was successful, the CLT is also not brought back into account. As no other gifts were made by A before his death, the full NRB is available to offset the IHT due on the estate.

<u>Taper Relief</u>

Taper relief applies to failed PETs to reduce the amount of IHT payable where the collective PETs exceed the NRB applicable at the time of the death. Taper relief is payable on the balance of the collective PETs over the NRB. The effective rate of IHT that will apply to failed PETs is dependent on the length of time between the failed PET being made and the death of the donor. The applicable rates of IHT for failed PETs are as follows:

Period of years before death when gift was made	% reduction in IHT (Taper Relief)	IHT payable on gift above NRB
0-3 years	0%	40%
3-4 years	20%	32%
4-5 years	40%	24%
5-6 years	60%	16%
6-7 years	80%	8%
In excess of 7 years	N/A	N/A

Business Property Relief (BPR)

This is a relief which applies to reduce the IHT due on certain business assets. In order to qualify for the relief, the deceased must have held the asset upon which relief is sought for a minimum of two years prior to their death. Once the time frame qualification has been met, the relief can apply at either 50% or 100%.

100% relief will operate on:

- A business or interest in a business; or

- Shares in an unlisted (privately owned) business

50% relief will operate on:

- A shareholding in a listed (publicly owned) company which controls more than 50% of the voting rights in the company

- Land, buildings and/or machinery owned by the deceased and which was used in a business in which they were a partner or otherwise controlled

- Land, buildings and/or machinery used in a business and which is held in a trust that the business has the right to benefit from

It is important to note that in respect of business interests, the business must be a fully trading business. A business which consists of activities that are wholly or mainly related to making investments will not qualify for the relief. A property investment business will (more than likely) be a business which is considered to be one which consists wholly or mainly of making investments and will not qualify for the relief. By comparison, a business which is a retail enterprise is likely on the face of it to qualify for the relief. A business such as a nursery which owns its own building is also likely to qualify for the relief for while it owns its own building, the majority to the activities within the business are trading activities and the ownership of the building is an incidental rather than a main trading activity. The key point to note is that each business will turn on its own facts as to whether it qualifies for the relief. There is a myriad of case law on this point which will be useful if you find yourself staring down the barrel of an argument with HMRC over whether the business is a trading business or one consisting of wholly or mainly making investments.

BPR can apply for gifts made within 7 years of the death of the original owner. In order to qualify for the relief, the recipient must have continued to hold the asset in a business context from the date of gift to the date of death (although certain property can be replaced such as machinery so long as it is of equal value and continues to be used in the business during the relevant period) and the deceased must have owned the asset for two years prior to making the gift.

Agricultural Property Relief (APR)

This is predominantly land used for farming purposes but also includes ancillary items such as farmhouses and land subject to grazing leases. This relief has a two or seven-year qualification period. The two-year period applies where the land is physically occupied by the owner, the owner's business or the owner's spouse or civil partner for agricultural purposes. The seven-year period applies where the land is occupied by someone else for agricultural purposes.

This should be, on the face of it, a straightforward relief – either you qualify or you don't. There is however a huge raft of case law on what can qualify under the legislation. Farmhouses are likely to be the biggest thing that will cause you angst over whether they will qualify. They must be occupied by the deceased, a farm employee or certain connected relations and must be of a nature and size appropriate to farming activities so large farmhouses on a small farm are going to cause (and have caused if the case law is anything to go by!) difficulties.

You cannot claim both BPR and APR on an asset and therefore as BPR is (usually) the relief that will provide the highest amount of relief, in circumstances where both reliefs would apply, you would normally elect to claim BPR rather than APR.

Spousal Exemption

As with gifts in life, all legacies and shares of residue left to spouses/civil partners on death will be exempt from IHT as long as they meet the residence and marriage conditions.

Grossing

Where there is no direction as to who should pay the IHT on legacies, the IHT due will be born by the legatee.

Example

A dies with a net estate worth £1.2m. A leaves a gift to their friend B of £400,000 and the residue to A's spouse, C. No gifts were made in the 7 years before A's death. The tax on £400,000 would be £400,000 – (£400,000-£325,000 = £75,000 * 40%) = £30,000. B therefore receives £370,000 (£400,000-£30,000) and C receives £800,000.

However, where the legacy is left free of IHT, this means that the legatee will need to receive the amount stated in the Will rather than the amount stated less the IHT due. The effect of this is that the exempt beneficiaries will receive less from the estate than they otherwise would have done had the legacy been subject to IHT. A calculation has to be done to gross up the legacy to take account of the IHT due.

Example

A dies with a net estate worth £1.2m. A leaves a gift to their friend B of £400,000 free of IHT and the residue to A's spouse, C. No gifts were made in the 7 years before A's death. B's legacy is calculated as follows:

Legacy per Will	£400,000
LESS: NRB	£325,000
Taxable element	£ 75,000

£75,000 x (100/60)   =   £125,000 + £325,000 (NRB)
= £450,000 = grossed up legacy

C will receive £750,000 as residue which is £50,000 less than C would have received had B's legacy been subject to IHT rather than net of IHT.

You can cross check this calculation (and when it comes to IHT, cross checking is always essential as the tax has the propensity to fry even the most spectacular of tax brains!) by checking the amount of tax due on the grossed up legacy and deducting it from the grossed up legacy. The answer should equal the legacy per the Will.

Example

Per the above example, £450,000 - £325,000 (NRB) = £125,00 x 40% = £50,000 IHT due. £450,000 - £50,000 IHT due = £400,000 which equals the legacy.

CHAPTER NINETEEN

INCOME TAX

Income tax will apply up to the date of the deceased's death and also for the period of administration of the estate.

<u>Date of Death</u>

You will need to finalise the deceased's Income Tax position to date of death. To this end, when undertaking the initial investigations into the extent of the estate, you should ask for details of the income and the tax deducted (if any) from the assets for the tax year in which the deceased died and the preceding tax year. You should also ask HMRC for a copy of the deceased's last tax return (if they filed one).

If the deceased had an accountant, the Executors can employ the accountant to bring all matters up to date. The accountants' expenses will be a legitimate expense of the administration of the estate. In any event, you will need to provide the accountant with details of the relevant income.

Where there is no accountant or where the deceased did not have to complete a self-assessment tax return (SA100) (for example, where all tax was deducted at source), then you will need to make sure that the deceased has paid the right amount of tax to date of death. Where the deceased has paid too much tax, a refund will be due to the estate.

It used to be the case that you would fill in a short form tax return for a deceased person which would confirm the tax due to or by the estate. Some years ago, HMRC did away with this procedure and work out the tax due to or by the estate from the information they have received from asset holders through real time reporting. This was apparently to do away with the errors made by lay Executors. However the fatal flaw in this particular plan is that it does not take account of chargeable events which can affect the amount of Income Tax due on an estate.

What is a chargeable event?

A chargeable event can occur when money is taken out of an investment bond. An investment bond is generally a single premium whole of life policy which has an investment value which can rise and fall like any other stock market related product. While the chargeable event is triggered by a gain arising on liquidation, the tax charge that applies is Income Tax rather than Capital Gains Tax[109]. A chargeable event can be triggered by the following types of events;

1. Death of the policy holder where the death gives rise to a benefit;

2. Assignment of all rights under the policy for money or money's worth;

3. Maturity of the investment bond;

4. Partial surrender or assignments;

5. Policy loans;

6. Surrender of all rights under the policy; or

7. Reclassification of the bond as a personal portfolio bond;

Death of the policy holder will only trigger a chargeable event where the death triggers a benefit e.g. the bond comes to an end on the death. If a bond is taken out on a joint life, second death basis, there will be no chargeable event on the first death as the bond does not end on the first death but there will be a chargeable event on the second death as the bond will terminate at that time.

It is important to understand the reasons which will trigger a chargeable event to avoid a chargeable event arising unnecessarily during the administration of the estate when you go to realise the bond.

---

[109] S461 (1) Income Tax (Trading and Other Income) Act (ITTOIA) 2005

A gift of a bond will not trigger a chargeable event unless cash or assets are exchanged. It is therefore possible to assign out some or all of the bond to non or lower rate taxpayers without triggering a chargeable event. The beneficiary can thereafter encash their share of the bond which may trigger a chargeable event which will be payable at that beneficiary's marginal rate of tax. This means that you can effectively manage the amount of tax which will be paid and avoid triggering excess tax to be paid within the estate.

Partial surrenders can trigger a chargeable event. Under the bond rules, you can withdraw up to 5% of the capital settled into the bond per year without triggering an immediate charge to tax. If you withdraw more than 5% of the capital in the one year, it will trigger a chargeable event.

Example

A settled £100,000 into an investment bond on 1 January 2017.

A draws down £9,000 on 30 July 2018.

A can drawdown £5,000 per tax year without triggering an immediate charge to tax.

As no drawdowns were made in the first year, the first year's unused £5,000 carries forward to the second year giving a total available drawdown of £10,000 without triggering a chargeable event.

As the £9,000 drawn down is less than the available £10,000, no chargeable event occurs on the draw down.

A then wishes to draw down a further £9,000 on 25 September 2019. The total available allowance before triggering a chargeable event will be £5,000 (year 1) + £5,000 (year 2) + £5,000 (year 3) − £9,000 (year 2) = £6,000. If A draws down the £9,000 in 2019, there will be a gain and therefore a chargeable event of £3,000 (£9,000 − £6,000) on the draw down. This can be avoided if A takes £6,000 or less from the bond on 25 September 2019.

If at the 1 January 2019, A invested a further £200,000 into the bond, the available allowance for the 25 September 2019 drawdown would be as follows:

Year 1 (1 January 2017 – 31 December 2017) = £5,000
(5% of Settlement 1 of £100,000)

Year 2 (1 January 2018 – 31 December 2018) = £5,000
(5% of Settlement 1 of £100,000)

Year 3 (1 January 2019 – 31 December 2019) = £15,000
(5% of Settlement 1 of £100,000 + 5% of Settlement 2 of £200,000)

Less

Withdrawal Year 2 (1 January 2018 – 31 December 2018) = £9,000
(Settlement 1)

Equals

Available allowance of £16,000.

As the available allowance of £16,000 exceeds the second proposed draw down of £9,000 in year 3, the second £9,000 could be drawn down without triggering a chargeable event.

A dies on 30 January 2021. As it was a single life assured bond, the bond comes to an end, and a chargeable event will arise on death.

If it had been a joint life, second death bond between A & B, there would be no chargeable event on A's death.

Income Tax for the period of administration

You will also need to ensure that all Income Tax is paid during the period of administration of the estate.

Informal Method

This can be done informally with HMRC through a letter, production of your Income Tax calculation along with a cheque for the tax you have calculated to be due where the following conditions apply:

1. The estate at date of death was worth less than £2.5m;

2. Estate realised in the tax year that you are dealing with is £500,000 or less; and

3. The total Income Tax and Capital Gains Tax for the tax year you are dealing with is less than £10,000

Formal Method

Where one or more of these conditions is not met, you will need to submit a formal tax return (SA900). As with the tax to date of death, you may wish to employ an accountant to do this for you. If you do not have an accountant employed in the estate, you will need to register the estate for Income Tax before you can submit the tax return at https://www.gov.uk/guidance/register-your-clients-estate You will need an agent services account to be able to register your client's estate. If you do not have one, you can create one the first time that you go to register an estate. Bear in mind that if you need to obtain an agent services account log in id, you will need a couple of weeks for the log in details to be received so make sure you leave enough time to obtain one against the deadlines for registration.

The deadline for registering an estate with HMRC is 5 October in the tax year after the tax year that you require to submit the tax return for.

Example

If you require to declare underpaid tax for the tax year 2020/2021 then you will need to register the estate by 5 October 2021.

Once your estate is registered with HMRC, HMRC will issue a unique taxpayer reference (UTR) for the estate which will need to be quoted on the tax return.

Tax Rate

Estates are taxed at the basic rate of tax as applied by the Westminster Government.

ISA

ISA income is taxed differently to the rest of the estate income. As with the position before death, for the first 3 years post death, any income and gains remain tax free within the estate.

R185e

Where income arises in an estate, you will need to notify the residuary beneficiaries of their share of the income and the tax paid thereon as they will need to report the income on their tax return. Where the beneficiary is a higher rate taxpayer, they will need to pay the difference between the tax paid by the estate and the tax due as a higher rate taxpayer. Likewise where the beneficiary is a non or lower rate taxpayer, they can reclaim the tax paid by the estate on their behalf. The income is reported annually by the Executors using form R185e[110].

---

[110] https://assets.publishing.service.gov.uk/government/uploads/system/uploads/attachment_data/file/603950/R185_Estate_Income__03_17.pdf

CHAPTER TWENTY

CAPITAL GAINS
TAX

Capital Gains Tax (CGT) does apply to estates but not in the same way as it does to individuals. You therefore need to check whether any disposal of an asset during the administration of the estate triggers a gain that needs to be reported.

If you are not confident in calculating the tax that may be due in the estate, you should outsource to either the deceased's accountant (if they had one) or a reputable accountant whom you have encountered through your networking. You may also have an inhouse tax department who can assist you with the tax calculation.

Your principal goal here should be to identify if you have a tax problem and what steps need to be taken to identify the same. The last thing you need is for tax issue to arise post wind up and distribution of the estate whereby the Executor will be personally liable for settling the liability and will thereafter be looking towards your indemnity policy for restitution if this is something which should have been within your foresight to deal with.

<u>When does CGT arise?</u>

CGT will be triggered when an asset is sold at a gain from its acquisition cost. For estates, the acquisition cost of an asset is uplifted to the date of death value, regardless of when it was originally purchased by the deceased and the price paid. It is therefore important that you keep this in mind when getting assets valued at date of death as the value attributed to the asset not only determines the Inheritance Tax that is due on the estate but also the base cost for establishing any subsequent gains and losses on the estate.

If your estate crosses several tax years, it is sensible to keep a record of what assets are sold in each tax year to calculate whether CGT will become payable.

Annual allowance

The annual allowance which applies to an estate is the same as the annual allowance which applies to individuals which at the time of writing this book was £12,300[111]. The allowance tends to move annually by a few hundred pounds. You can check current and historic annual allowances at https://www.gov.uk/guidance/capital-gains-tax-rates-and-allowances# tax-free-allowances-for-capital-gains-tax The CGT annual allowance is a use it or lose it relief – if it is not utilised during the applicable tax year, it cannot be carried forward to the next year allow though losses can be.

There is however one very important difference between CGT for estates and individuals and that is the length of time that an annual allowance will apply to estates. Individuals annual allowance renews every year for the lifetime of the individual. For estates, Executors only have an annual allowance for the three years following the death. Thereafter no annual allowance applies to any disposals of assets. The effect of this is that if assets continue to be held in the estate following the expiry of the three tax years, there will be no annual allowance to offset any gains made. It is therefore in everyone's interests to realise assets as far as possible within the first three tax years to take advantage of the annual allowance to minimise the tax that needs to be paid by the estate.

The three years allowance runs from the date of death. Depending on where the deceased died in the tax year, the first year's allowance may not be capable of being utilised.

Example

Mr A dies on 3 March 2020. The tax years that will carry the Executors annual allowance are:

---

[111] November 2022

1. 2020/2021

2. 2021/2022

3. 2022/2023

As you will only have 33 days of the 2020/2021 tax year left following the death, it is unlikely that your Executors will be in a position to utilise the allowance and it is essentially lost. The net effect of this is that practically speaking, the Executor only has two years annual allowance to use.

Example

Mr B dies on 6 April 2020. The tax years that will carry the Executors annual allowance are:

1. 2020/2021

2. 2021/2022

3. 2022/2023

Compared to foregoing example, the Executor will have almost 3 full years to administer the estate and take advantage of all three years allowances.

> **TIP** – where your deceased dies close to the expiry of the tax year and if based on your initial meeting and assessment of the paperwork presented, the estate is likely to be subject to Inheritance Tax and it contains a portfolio of shares, you may wish to consider whether you ought to have the Executors instruct the broker to sell down a sufficient part of the portfolio to utilise the CGT allowance for the tax year of the date of death. Most discretionary fund manager (DFM) houses will allow you to do so ahead of Probate being granted where the ultimate recipient of the funds is going to be HMRC. They will normally require an undertaking from the Executors to put them back into the position they would have been in had they not acted on the instruction – for example, where a competing Executor arises or ultimately it is found that your Executor does not have the title to authorise the sale. Depending on the extent of the Inheritance Tax due, you may not need to utilise the whole allowance to raise the funds from the portfolio but you should certainly consider whether you should do so to take advantage of all allowances particularly if the death occurs at a time of rising markets where the portfolio may be subject to a gain even a short time after the death. Needless to say, the DFM's will not usually release the funds to HMRC until they have sight of a copy of the IHT400.

Deductible Allowances

Aside from the annual allowance, it is also possible to reduce the gain due on an estate by deducting certain allowances. All of the available allowances that can apply to the estate are outwith the remit of this book. Suffice it to say, if you have a particularly complicated transaction such as the sale of farmland which is being sold to developers and for which may take several years to negotiate a sale and incur a myriad of expenses in the interim, employ an accountant to ensure that the estate does not pay more tax than it should.

Rates of CGT

The rate of CGT that will apply to each transaction will depend on the asset being sold. The applicable rates of CGT for Executors at the time of writing this book[112] are as follows:

1. For disposals of land and property, the rate of CGT is 28%

2. For all other assets, such as shares, stamp collections etc, the rate of CGT is 20%

The rates do change from time to time (for example, in November 2022, the Chancellor has announced a radical reduction to the CGT annual allowance commencing in 2023) so ensure you check the applicable rates for the relevant tax year on HMRC's website.

Please note that this is different to the rates which apply to individuals in life.

How to report CGT

You can use the informal method to report CGT to HMRC where **all** of the following circumstances apply:

1. The value of the estate at date of death was less than £2.5m;

2. The total Income Tax and Capital Gains Tax for the applicable tax year totals less than £10,000; and

3. The total amount of assets realised within the current tax year does not exceed £500,000

The informal method is simply to write to HMRC with the name of the deceased, their national insurance number, a copy of your calculation, a statement in your covering letter which confirms that all of the above conditions apply, a request to deal with the tax position for the administration of the estate to be dealt with under the informal method

---

[112] November 2022

and a cheque for the tax due. If the estate concluded within the tax year you are writing to HMRC about, you should also confirm that in your letter with a request to close off the estate's records. HMRC will normally write back to confirm acceptance of the position or they will raise queries.

In the event that your estate does not meet all of the above conditions, it will be necessary for you to register the estate for self-assessment. This is now done online via https://www.gov.uk/guidance/register-your-clients-estate

The estate must be registered online by the 5 October after the tax year when the estate starts to receive income or has chargeable gains on which tax is payable. HMRC will thereafter issue the estate with a Unique Taxpayer Reference (also known as an UTR) which will used to file the tax return.

In order to register the estate, you will need the following information to register the estate:

- The deceased's name

- The deceased's last known address

- The deceased's date of birth

- The deceased's date of death

- The deceased's National Insurance number (if available)

- The name of the estate, for example, "The estate of Joseph Bloggs, deceased"

- An address for the estate and contact telephone number (this will usually be the lead Executor's address and number)

- The Executor's name

- The Executor's address

- The Executor's date of birth

- The Executor's national insurance number (or passport number with expiry date)

- The Executor's telephone number and an email address

- If applicable, the date the administration period ended.

You can file a paper return up to 31 October in the tax year following the tax year in which the gain was triggered or you have until 31 January of the next year to file the return online. You will need an agent services account if you want to file online. This can be created at https://www.access.service.gov.uk/login/signin/creds.

All tax due will in any event be payable by 31 January of the year following the tax year that you are reporting on.

CHAPTER TWENTY-ONE

CONTESTING ESTATES

While a testator has freedom to dispose of their estate as they see fit, there are certain claims which can be lodged which can vary the disposal of the deceased's estate from that which was intended (or in certain cases, unintended!).

Grounds of Contest

The common grounds of contest of an estate are as follows:

1. Want of due execution of the Will

2. Lack of capacity

3. Want of knowledge and approval

4. Undue influence

5. Fraud

6. Inheritance (Provision for Family and Dependants) Act 1975 Claims

7. Proprietary Estoppel claims

Want of due execution

This would apply in situations where a Will has not been signed in the correct manner[113]. This can include errors in the way in which the Will was executed, for example, missing signatures or witnesses or where the testator is under 18 years old at the time of execution. It requires the

---

[113] S9 Wills Act 1837

"strongest evidence possible"[114]. Evidence from the Witnesses to the Will can and should be led and can be critical in the success or failure of such a claim[115].

The relatively recent case of Marley v Rawlings[116] considered various points on due execution in circumstances where a couple signed each other's Will in error and paved the way for rectification of the Will.

Lack of Capacity

This ground works on the premise that the testator lacked capacity to sign a Will at the time it was made and therefore there is not a valid Will. The test for capacity for signing a Will is laid out in Banks V Goodfellow[117] in what is now regarded as "the Golden Rule". The case confirms that the testator:

1. Must appreciate the nature and consequences of making a Will;

2. Must understand the extent of his or her property;

---

[114] Wright v Rogers [1869] LR 1 PD 678

[115] Burgess v Penny & Anr. [2019] EWHC 2034 (Ch) in which the Will appeared to be formally valid but was rebutted on the basis that one Witness to the Will had not seen either the deceased or the other witness sign. Also see Re Whelen [2015] EWHC 3301 in which the witnesses confirmed that while they had witnessed the signature being appended to the Will, it was that of the beneficiary rather than that of the purported testator.

[116] [2014] UKSC 2

[117] (1870) LR 5 QB 549. Banks V Goodfellow has been confirmed as remaining good law in Walker v Badmin [2014] EWHC 71 (CH); [2015] WTLR 493, James v James [2018] EWHC 43 (Ch) and latterly in Clitheroe v Bond [2021] EWHC 1102 (Ch).

3. Should consider any moral claims to their estate; and

4. Must not be affected by any disorder of mind or insane delusion.

A valid Will may still be possible where the testator had capacity at the time of instruction on the Will but whose capacity had waned at the time of execution. In these circumstances it will need to be shown that the testator had sufficient capacity at the time of execution of the Will to understand that they were signing a Will which they had previously instructed[118].

Want of Knowledge and Approval

This action often goes hand in hand with a lack of capacity action as if the testator lacked capacity, they would not have been capable of knowing and approving the contents of the Will presented before them. It is however a distinct ground of action from capacity as the testator can have capacity but not qualify under the knowledge and approval of the document[119]. With questions of capacity, the test is whether the testator is <u>capable</u> of understanding the terms of the Will and the consequences of their instruction to prepare the Will on the instructed terms. With knowledge and approval, the test is whether the Testator <u>actually knew and approved</u> of the contents of the Will that was signed.

It can also be raised in circumstances where it is thought that a fraud has occurred. Where a Will has been forged, the testator cannot have had knowledge and approval of the contents of the Will[120] as it was not instructed by them nor signed by them. The burden of proof is on the person relying on the Will at hand to prove that the Will is the last true Will of the deceased[121].

---

[118] Parker V Felgate (1883) 8 PD 171

[119] Hoff V Atherton [2005]WTLR 99

[120] Re Rowinska, Wyniczenko V Plucinska-Sorowka [2006] WTLR 487

[121] Barry V Butlin [1838] UKPC 22

Undue Influence

Undue influence refers to situations in which the execution of the Will is as a consequence of the influence of one or more individuals. Undue influence can be difficult to prove as the acts leading up to the execution of the Will will often be undertaken in private without witnesses. Cases will usually turn on the facts and circumstances of establishing the:

1. nature of the relationship between the testator and the person(s) attempting to overcome the Will of the testator;

2. nature of the transactions that have taken place during the lifetime of the testator including the execution of the Will at the centre of the litigation;

3. presence of Coercion as it will affect the testator's intention to make a Will[122].

The burden of proof is on the person raising the action to show that a decision was made by the testator as a consequence of the influence of one or more other individuals.

Fraud

This occurs in situations where the Will was obtained through deception. This can be as simple as the presentation of a forged Will or it can be more complex, for example, where the testator has been fed information which causes them to have a false interpretation of the facts which results in a person being unduly favoured or indeed disinherited in the Will. This is an extremely difficult action to prove as much like undue influence, many of the acts which lead up to a Will being executed as result of fraud occur in private.

---

[122] Wingrove V Wingrove (1886) 11 PD 81

Inheritance (Provision for Family and Dependants) Act 1975 Claims

While Testators have of course the freedom to leave their assets to whomsoever they wish, the Inheritance (Provision for Family and Dependants) Act 1975 provides a mechanism for disappointed familial beneficiaries to make a claim against the estate – the ground for a claim is that reasonable financial provision has not been made for the claimant. This can also be used in intestate cases where the division of the estate on intestacy fails to make reasonable provision for the claimant.

Examples of reasonable provision not being made can include the exclusion of a spouse or child from deriving any benefit from the estate.

What is reasonable financial provision?

It should be noted here that the 'reasonableness' test turns on what the Judge determines is reasonable and not on what the deceased thought was reasonable – no matter if what the deceased deemed was reasonable was what drove the deceased to draft his Will in the form which is now being contested.

The Court is at liberty to consider all of the facts available at the time the application for reasonable financial provision is made. As you will appreciate, this can include facts and circumstances which the deceased may have been unaware of at the time of instructing his Will which had he otherwise known about, may or may not have made a difference to the division of the estate. Hindsight is 20/20 as they say!

There is a higher standard for making provision for a spouse[123] than there is for any other possible claimant[124].

---

[123] S1(2)(a) and S1(2)(aa) Inheritance (Provision for Family & Dependants) Act 1975 provides that the standard is what is reasonable for a spouse to have regardless of whether such provision is needed for their maintenance.

[124] Such provision in these cases will be what is reasonable for their maintenance only.

Who can claim?

The claimant must fall into one of the following categories:

1. A spouse or civil partner of the deceased;

2. A former spouse or civil partner of the deceased that has not remarried;

3. Any child of the deceased;

4. Any person who is treated as if they were a child of the deceased e.g. a step child, a foster child, a niece or nephew who the deceased looked after as their Guardian etc.

5. Any person who was being financially provided for by the deceased in whole or in part e.g. where the deceased's adult sibling lived with them and they were housed and given an allowance or the deceased met school fees for a niece or nephew etc

The legitimacy or otherwise of a child does not affect their ability to make a claim using this mechanism.

Where the death occurred on or after 1 January 1996, a claim can also be made by a person who lived in the same household as the deceased as if they were the spouse of the deceased as long as cohabitation on these terms took place during the whole of the two years immediately preceding the death[125].

How to claim

To make a successful claim, all of the following must apply:

1. The claimant falls within one of the categories listed above;

2. The deceased must have died domiciled in England & Wales;

---

[125] S1(1A) Inheritance (Provision for Family & Dependants) Act 1975

3. The claim illustrates why the intestate position or the provision in the Will (or lack thereof as the case may be) does not provide reasonable financial provision for the claimant; and

4. The claim must be lodged within 6 months of the first Grant of Probate/Letters of Administration being granted.

It is important to note that if the claimant also dies before the Court makes a decision, the claim also dies with them. The ability to pursue the claim does not pass to their executors[126].

Intimation of Late Claims

There is the possibility to admit a late claim[127] post 6 months after the Grant has been made however the burden of proof is on the claimant to prove the special circumstances as to why an extension should be granted e.g. A child not being notified of the death in a timely manner. In considering the admission of a late claim, the Court needs to consider the following:

1. The speed at which the application has been made after the Grant has been issued;

2. The circumstances which caused a late application to be submitted;

3. The chain of communication that occurred in the 6 months from the Grant between the claimant and the personal representatives (if any);

4. Would refusal to allow an extension leave the claimant without any other avenue of recourse e.g. the deceased died testate and it was a negligently drafted Will which caused the lack of reasonable financial provision to occur?

---

[126] Whyte V Ticehurst (1986) 2 All ER 158

[127] See Re Salmon (dec'd) [1980] Ch 167 and Re Dennis [1981] 2 All ER 140

5. Has the estate already been distributed?

<u>Factors to be considered</u>

On hearing a claim, the Judge will have regard to the following factors[128]:

1. The current and future financial needs and resources of the claimant, any other claimants and actual beneficiaries of the estate may have;

2. Any obligations or responsibilities which the deceased had to the claimant, any other claimants and actual beneficiaries of the estate;

3. the value and composition of the estate;

4. any other matter which the Judge may consider relevant given the particular circumstances of the case. This can also include consideration of the conduct of the claimant;

Where the claimant is or was a spouse of the deceased, the Court will also consider:

1. The age of the claimant;

2. The length of the marriage;

3. The status of the relationship between the deceased and the claimant e.g. were they separated? Was a financial separation agreement in place at the time of the death?

4. The contribution to the family unit made by the claimant. This does not need to be a financial contribution. It can also include a contribution of unpaid but equally as important work, for example, where a spouse has given up in full or in part a career to

---

[128] S3 Inheritance (Provision for Family and Dependants) Act 1975

be a care giver to children of the relationship or to look after the deceased;

It is well worth your while to read all of the case reports in the well-publicised case of Ilott V Mitson[129] which involved a claim by a daughter who had been estranged from her Mother for 26 years and the Mother had favoured leaving provision for her estate to a number of charities. While provision was eventually made in favour of the daughter notwithstanding that the Mother had not been involved in maintaining the daughter during her lifetime, the case history illustrates how difficult and costly it can be to obtain provision for a non-spouse.

Outcome of a Claim

If a claim is successful, the Court can order provision to be made in the following forms;

1. A single lump sum;

2. periodic payments;

3. delivering of one or more assets in satisfaction of the claim;

4. a settlement; or

5. the variation of an existing settlement including pre or post nuptial agreements[130]

Proprietary Estoppel

This is a ground of challenge whereby the testator makes a number of representations to an individual (the disappointed beneficiary) that causes the individual to react in a way that is to his or her financial detriment in relation to land and property. This usually takes the form of the testator promising on multiple occasions that their house or farm

---

[129] [2015] EWCA Civ 797 and [2017] UKSC 17

[130] Roberts & Anor V Fresco [2017] EWHC 283 (Ch)

will become the disappointed beneficiary's on the death of the testator if they undertake certain actions. On the death of the testator, the land is divested to someone other than disappointed beneficiary.

In order to bring a successful claim, the claimant must meet the following tests[131]:

1. that a representation or assurance has been made to the claimant;

2. that the claimant has relied on it; and

3. that the claimant has suffered a detriment as a result of the reliance

There has to be more than a person simply saying they have an intention to do a certain thing[132] then not following through. These cases will very much turn on the facts and circumstances of each individual case. There is no defined remedy for a claim under this provision – the Court will consider the circumstances of each case and then consider what is equitable in the circumstances to right the wrong that has been done. This may include enforcing the promise or making an award in favour of the hitherto disappointed beneficiary

---

[131] Thorner V Major [2009] UKHL 18

[132] James v James 2018 EWHC 43 (Ch)

CHAPTER TWENTY-TWO

BUSINESS DEVELOPMENT OPPORTUNITIES

The administration of the estate does not need to be the end of the business. There are a number of additional services which can be offered by your practice which can enhance the income generating opportunities from having an enhanced private client practice.

Business Development Opportunities Arising from an Estate

Deeds of Variation

As you circulate the schedule of assets during the administration of the estate prior to obtaining Probate, it is useful to raise the possibility of granting a Deed of Variation as often beneficiaries do not appreciate that they can vary their entitlement. This can then lead to a conversation regarding Inheritance Tax planning, succession planning, Wills and protecting assets against incapacity which then introduces the beneficiary as a new client to your firm.

Will review

You can also offer to review beneficiaries Wills during the administration of the estate to ensure that it continues to fit with the person's financial and family circumstances in light of their inheritance. Alternatively, you can offer to write a Will should they not have one. It is useful to offer this service prior to distributions being made as often clients are more likely to take advantage of this service where they do not physically have to pay you any money from their own pocket and the fees can be deducted from their share of the estate.

Power of Attorney

As with Wills, it is worthwhile asking about Powers of Attorney. As any good private client practitioner recognises, Powers of Attorney should be part of an individual's overall wealth management strategy. All too often, clients only come to us when Mum has been diagnosed with dementia or otherwise where incapacity has already struck in which case it a lengthier application to the Court of Protection for Deputyship. A Power of Attorney is not just for the elderly and should be marketed accordingly.

Financial Advice

Beneficiaries of estates can inherit significant amounts of money. It is always worthwhile suggesting that they take independent financial advice. You may wish to make contact with a number of financial advisers who you can use for this type of business. That way, if your client wishes to take financial advice and they do not have an existing adviser, you can provide details of the various financial advisers that you work with and suggest to the client that they call round the advisers so that they can decide if they wish to take financial advice and which adviser they feel most comfortable with. Be sure to check whether the financial adviser is an independent or tied adviser and confirm with the beneficiary accordingly. Tied advisers will be restricted to the products of one or more investment companies. An independent financial adviser will be able to select the best products for the client from all of the available products and investment companies on the market. In turn, you may find that the financial advisers will start to introduce new clients to you.

Cross Department Private Client Business Development Opportunities

Conveyancing

Where a conveyancing transaction is being undertaken, it is always worthwhile the conveyancer asking the question if the person has a Will or Power of Attorney. If not, there is an opportunity for you to put one in place. Where there are existing documents in place, it is also an opportunity for you to review them to make sure that they still fit with the person's financial and family circumstances. The only thing worse than having no Will is having a Will which is outdated and which lands assets with entirely the wrong people.

Conveyancing/Family Law

If the firm are acting in the purchase of a property involving a cohabiting couple, recommend that they put a Will in place which at least covers what happens to the house in the event of the death of one of them. The last thing a person needs on the death of their partner is to discover they are co-owners with an in-law:

1. They don't get on with;

2. Who insists on being bought out of the property which could bring financial hardship to the surviving partner;

3. Who forces a sale of the property where the cohabiting partner can't buy them out so the surviving partner loses both their house and their partner; or

4. Who insists on moving in beside the partner!

Likewise, it is always worth recommending that a cohabitation agreement is put in place when the couple are buying a house (or indeed moving in together in general). While no one hopes that a relationship will end, having a cohabitation agreement in place can at least make the financial aspects of the separation relatively straight forward leaving "only" the emotional fall out to be dealt with. This is particularly important where one party is bringing more in wealth to the relationship then the other for example, the deposit from a sale of their previous property or a contribution from the Bank of Mum and Dad. This will go some way to ensuring that the person bringing the additional funds does not lose out in the event of the need for a subsequent sale or transfer on separation. In this case, both parties will need to have the ability to access independent financial and legal advice but if one person has insufficient funds to take that advice (usually the person bringing the smaller value of assets to the relationship/purchase), this can be covered by the wealthier party by insertion of a clause into the agreement confirming a restricted agreed contribution towards their partner's costs, say £250-300 plus VAT (or whatever the going rate is in your area for say an hour/hour and a half's solicitor's time).

Push back on cohabitation agreements is usually the costs and enforceability of the agreement. The counter argument to that is that spending a few hundred pounds now will be far less than it will cost to reach a financial settlement in the event of a separation further down the line.

Immigration Law

Particularly in these post-Brexit times, it is important to check the residence status of spouses/civil partners, cohabiting partners and children. Where it is found that someone is not a British National and their right to live in the UK was dependant on their relationship with the deceased, that person may have to apply for a new visa and they may require help in navigating the visa system. There are also different rules which will apply where the deceased died as a member of the armed forces.

Further information can be found at https://www.gov.uk/contact-ukvi-inside-outside-uk

CHAPTER TWENTY-THREE

USEFUL ADDRESSES
AND CONTACT DETAILS

(correct as at December 2022

<u>Banks</u>

<u>Bank of Scotland, Lloyds Bank, Halifax and MBNA</u>

<u>https://www.bankofscotland.co.uk/helpcentre/bereavement.html</u>

<u>Royal Bank of Scotland</u>

<u>https://www.rbs.co.uk/life-moments/bereavement.html#notify</u>

<u>TSB</u>

<u>https://www.tsb.co.uk/help-and-support/bereavement-and-coping-with-loss/#letting-us-know</u>

<u>Santander</u>

<u>https://bereavement-online.santander.co.uk/bereavement-frontend/index</u>

<u>Barclays</u>

<u>https://www.barclays.co.uk/what-to-do-when-someone-dies/notify-us/</u>

<u>Company Registrars</u>

<u>Equiniti</u>

<u>https://www.shareview.co.uk/4/Info/Portfolio/default/en/home/shareholders/BereavementSupport/Pages/Bereavement-Support.aspx</u>

Computershare Investor Services PLC

The Pavilions
Bridgwater Road
Bristol
BS99 6ZZ

Link Asset Services

https://ww2.linkassetservices.com/bereavement/

Genealogists

Estate Research

102 Chapel Lane
Wigan
WN3 4HG
DX: 19316 Wigan
E: info@estateresearch.co.uk
T: 01942 826500

Fraser and Fraser

39 Hatton Garden
London
EC1N 8EH
DX: 53304 Clerkenwell
E: info@fraserandfraser.co.uk
T: +44 (0) 20 7832 1400
F: +44 (0) 20 7832 1450

Finders International

83 Princes Street
Edinburgh
EH2 2ER
E: contact@findersinternational.co.uk

T: +44 (0) 131 278 0552
F: +44 (0)131 278 0548

Title Research

Spectrum House
Bond Street
Bristol
BS1 3LG
E: info@titleresearch.com
T: +44 (0) 345 87 27 600
F: +44 (0) 117 981 1474

Government Agencies

HMRC

Inheritance Tax
HM Revenue and Customs
BX9 1HT
T: 0300 123 1072

Department for Work and Pensions

To confirm if there are sums due to or by the estate:

Debt Management (RES)
Mail Handling Site A
Wolverhampton
WV98 2DH

For information relating to state benefits claimed by the deceased including tax information:

The Pension Service
Post Handling Site A
Wolverhampton
WV98 1AF

DVLA

https://www.gov.uk/tell-dvla-about-bereavement

Passport Office

https://www.gov.uk/government/publications/what-to-do-with-a-passport-when-the-passport-holder-has-died

Probate Registry

Leeds District Probate Registry
York House
31 York Place
Leeds
LS1 2BA
T: 0300 3030 648
E: leedsdprenquiries@justice.gov.uk

Brighton District Probate Registry
William Street
Brighton
BN2 0RF
E: brightondprenquiries@justice.gov.uk

Cardiff Probate Registry of Wales
3rd Floor, Cardiff Magistrates Court
Fitzalan Place
Cardiff
CF24 0RZ
E: cardiffdprenquiries@justice.gov.uk

Liverpool Probate Registry
Queen Elizabeth II Law Courts
Derby Square
Liverpool
L2 1XA
E: liverpooldprenquiries@justice.gov.uk

Newcastle District Probate Registry
2nd Floor
Kings Court
Earl Grey Way
North Shields
NE29 6AR
E: newcastledprenquiries@justice.gov.uk

Oxford Probate Registry
Combined Court Building
St Aldates
Oxford
OX1 1LY
E: oxforddprenquiries@justice.gov.uk

Winchester District Probate Registry
1st Floor, Southside Offices
The Law Courts
Winchester
SO23 9EL
E: winchesterdprenquiries@justice.gov.uk

The Central Chancery of the Orders of Knighthood

St James Palace
Marlborough Road
St. James's
London
SW1A 1BS

CHAPTER TWENTY-FOUR

FURTHER READING

This is by no means an exclusive list as there are lots of texts out there concerning the laws of succession in England and Wales. The following reflects my view on the basics that you should either have in your private client library or otherwise have access to from your local law library if you are wanting to build an estates practice within your firm. These books will in turn lead you on elsewhere:

Succession Law

- "Parry & Kerridge: The Law of Succession", Kerridge. R, 13th Edition, Sweet & Maxwell

- "Williams, Mortimer & Sunnucks – Executors, Administrators and Probate" Learmouth.A and others, 21st Edition, Sweet & Maxwell

Drafting of Wills and interpretation

- "Parkers Will Precedents" Pickering.L, 10th Edition, Bloomsbury Press

- "Drafting Trust & Will Trusts – a Modern Approach", Kessler, J, 14th Edition, Sweet & Maxwell

- "Theobald on Wills" Learmouth A and others, 19th Edition, Sweet & Maxwell

Probate Procedure

- "Probate Practice Manual", Rees. D, Sweet & Maxwell as updated twice annually.

Tax

- "McCutcheon on Inheritance Tax", 7th Edition, Sweet & Maxwell as supplemented

- "Mellows Taxation for Executors and Trustees" LexisNexis (please note this publication is a loose-leaf subscription service publication which is updated three times per year so check you have the most up to date version)

Each of the following books published by Tolley/Lexis-Nexis referred to below are produced annually to take account of updates to law and practice. You should therefore check you have the correct year for the administration year in question.

- Tolley's Inheritance Tax 2022-2023

- Tolley's Income Tax 2022-2023

- Tolley's Capital Gains Tax 2022-2023

- Tolley's Tax Guide 2022-2023 (short blast guide to various taxes)

- Whillans Tax Tables 2022-2023

Journals

- Society of Trusts and Estates Practitioners (STEP) Journal

- Private Client Law Review

Cross jurisdictional estates

- "Anton on Private International Law", 3rd Edition, W Green

MORE BOOKS BY
LAW BRIEF PUBLISHING

A selection of our other titles available now:-

'A Practical Guide to Parental Alienation in Private and Public Law Children Cases' by Sam King QC & Frankie Shama
'Contested Heritage – Removing Art from Land and Historic Buildings' by Richard Harwood QC, Catherine Dobson, David Sawtell
'The Limits of Separate Legal Personality: When Those Running a Company Can Be Held Personally Liable for Losses Caused to Third Parties Outside of the Company' by Dr Mike Wilkinson
'A Practical Guide to Transgender Law' by Robin Moira White & Nicola Newbegin
'Artificial Intelligence – The Practical Legal Issues (2ⁿᵈ Edition)' by John Buyers
'A Practical Guide to Residential Freehold Conveyancing' by Lorraine Richardson
'A Practical Guide to Pensions on Divorce for Lawyers' by Bryan Scant
'A Practical Guide to Challenging Sham Marriage Allegations in Immigration Law' by Priya Solanki
'A Practical Guide to Legal Rights in Scotland' by Sarah-Jane Macdonald
'A Practical Guide to New Build Conveyancing' by Paul Sams & Rebecca East
'A Practical Guide to Defending Barristers in Disciplinary Cases' by Marc Beaumont
'A Practical Guide to Inherited Wealth on Divorce' by Hayley Trim
'A Practical Guide to Practice Direction 12J and Domestic Abuse in Private Law Children Proceedings' by Rebecca Cross & Malvika Jaganmohan
'A Practical Guide to Confiscation and Restraint' by Narita Bahra QC, John Carl Townsend, David Winch
'A Practical Guide to the Law of Forests in Scotland' by Philip Buchan
'A Practical Guide to Health and Medical Cases in Immigration Law' by Rebecca Chapman & Miranda Butler
'A Practical Guide to Bad Character Evidence for Criminal Practitioners by Aparna Rao
'A Practical Guide to Extradition Law post-Brexit' by Myles Grandison et al

These books and more are available to order online direct from the publisher at www.lawbriefpublishing.com, where you can also read free sample chapters. For any queries, contact us on 0844 587 2383 or mail@lawbriefpublishing.com.

Our books are also usually in stock at www.amazon.co.uk with free next day delivery for Prime members, and at good legal bookshops such as Wildy & Sons.

We are regularly launching new books in our series of practical day-to-day practitioners' guides. Visit our website and join our free newsletter to be kept informed and to receive special offers, free chapters, etc.

You can also follow us on Twitter at www.twitter.com/lawbriefpub.

Printed in Great Britain
by Amazon

44302481R00110